W9-BXD-629

Generational Poverty

An Economic Look at the Culture of the Poor

Adam Vass Gal

www.vernonpress.com

Vernon Press is an imprint of Vernon Art & Science Inc.

In the Americas:
Vernon Press
1000 N West Street,
Suite 1200, Wilmington,
Delaware 19801
United States

In the rest of the world:
Vernon Press
C/Sancti Espiritu 17,
Malaga, 29006
Spain

Library of Congress Control Number: 2014948971

ISBN 978-1-62273-018-6

Contents

Preface

After participating in the Big Brothers program of Middle Tennessee, I was curious as to how productive my involvement had been. My work could have produced an infinite number of results. There could have been little to no impact or I could have orchestrated an amazing change in child's life. As I type this, I honestly do not know which impression I actually had. I hope that it is somewhere near the second outcome, but fear that it is closer to the first. As an economist, I tend to be overly realistic and conservative with my expectations. With that said, I do anticipate that my results are somewhere in the middle of the two scenarios.

This book is going to be a social experiment and I am personally interested in the results. I certainly have my preconceived notions about how charity and handouts typically work. However, it is important to get your hands dirty and actually experience the other side of the spectrum if you want to truly understand it. Reading and debating is a wonderful learning tool, but it will always be secondary to experience. Remaining above the fray while explaining what lies beneath the surface is a major flaw in academia. I do not want to fall into that trap.

Like everyone that gets involved in Big Brothers Big Sisters, I did it to make a difference in a child's life. I may have been a bit younger and more idealistic at the time, but I would go through the program again today. I did not originally plan to write a book about it or look at it from an investigational perspective. Still, I do feel that this will be a helpful exercise and may even challenge some of the economic theory and "truths" that I have come to believe.

The impact (or lack thereof) I had on my "Little" will have no bearing on my personal experience or on my enthusiasm to take on another child in the future.This study is simply a case of an economist taking advantage of social experiment that was conducted by accident. It is now time to compile the results. Please do not base your decision to join a similar organization on whatever outcome is achieved by the end of this book. The Big Brothers program is a remarkable organization and certainly worthy of any time you can contribute. The results will certainly vary for every "Big", but I can promise that you will learn a lot and take away a wonderful relationship with a child in need. The economic impact is debatable, but the emotional results will be incredibly worthwhile.

In the interest of discretion, I have changed all of the names of everyone involved with the Big Brothers program. I feel comfortable using the names of my friends and family, but I want to protect everyone else being examined. While doing my interview with the family, they agreed to me writing a book about them. Still, the sensitive nature of the items discussed could cause issues in the future. My hope is that the integrity of my research will not interfere with the many friendships I have been fortunate to form.

Part I

Program and Family Introductions

Chapter 1

Big Brothers Big Sisters of Middle Tennessee

Big Brothers Big Sisters (in the future will be referred to as BBBS) is the nation's largest donor and volunteer supported mentoring network[1]. Their mission is "to provide children facing adversity with strong and enduring, professionally supported one-to-one relationships that change their lives for the better, forever." The organization is over 100 years old and has had a considerable amount of success with young people in the mentoring process. BBBS has compiled some of the positive results on their website. They concluded that children in the program are:

- more confident in their schoolwork performance
- able to get along better with their families
- 46% less likely to begin using illegal drugs
- 27% less likely to begin using alcohol
- 52% less likely to skip school

While each of the items listed is a wonderful achievement, this book will explore other more specific areas. Most of the studies conducted will be targeted at long-term progressions and success in life. My study will be relatively limited to my personal experience, but it will take into account the lives of several young adults that have completed or are currently participating in the program. The goal is to find out if the children in question have had significant changes in their lives and if those changes will be lasting.

The results listed above actually come from a study that was conducted in 1994 by Public / Private Ventures, an independent Philadelphia- based national research organization[2]. They interacted with 950 boys and girls from across the country that had participated in the program. The study focused on the first 18 months

[1] "We Are Here to Start Something." Big Brothers Big Sisters. N.p., N.d.

[2] Tierney, J.P., Grossman, J.B., and Resch, N.L. (1995) *Making a Difference: An Impact Study of Big Brothers Big Sisters.* Philadelphia: Public/Private Ventures

of the relationship between the Big and the Little. The demographics of the study showed that a large portion of Littles are minorities and most of them are poor. Generally, the children in the program are average students and almost all of them come from a single-parent home.

The statistical improvements by the children in this study are mostly positive. There were significant drops in drug use, alcohol use, and violence. However, there were mixed results in regard to academics and overall family life. While the child's relationship with their parent went virtually unchanged, there was a significant drop in reported incidents of the child lying to the parent. Also, there were significant improvements in the child's behavior at school. Skipping class (and skipping school) dropped dramatically. The troubling statistic is that grades and overall scholastic performance experienced minimal change. While improvement in behavior will serve a person well throughout his or her life, it is discouraging to see that the positive influence did not improve their grades. We will talk extensively about this issue throughout the book.

Demand for a Big is high and there is typically a waiting list in most parts of the country. My screening process was very easy, but thorough. I completed an application that went into my background and history. BBBS focuses on education, criminal activity and working career. They do a background check on each applicant before proceeding to the interview process. This portion was also very relaxed. BBBS was happy to talk to me and appreciative of my interest. They fulfilled their screening obligations and after two months I was paired with my Little.

The first year of the program is a bit stringent. You are expected to meet with your Little once or twice a month and you get a call from a counselor monthly. They talk to the child, the parent, and to you to address any concerns that may arise as well as answer questions. Each conversation is confidential, but the counselor may make suggestions to any of the three parties about the relationship. They have a good overall picture of how things are going and this insight is invaluable. After a year, the calls come quarterly, but they are still thorough. The program lasts until the child turns 18 (or if the Big or Little decide to stop it at any time), but you are certainly welcome to continue to meet with your Little for as long as you like.

BBBS started in 1904 when a New York City county clerk named Earnest Coulter started noticing more and more young boys coming through his courtroom. He began finding volunteers to start mentoring these boys. At about the same time, there was also a movement called Ladies of Charity starting to form. They were a Catholic organization that searched for mentors for young girls. These two organizations worked independently from each other until 1977 when they combined to form Big Brothers Big Sisters of America. Today the organization operates in all 50 states and in 12 different countries.

BBBS has a few areas where they provide a little extra attention. They deliver specialized care for children of Native American, African-American, Hispanic, and military homes. They also have an initiative called the Amachi Program. Amachi is a Nigerian word meaning "who knows but what God has brought us through this child." This particular program is for children that have an incarcerated parent. I was invited to work through this section of the organization, but also given the option to go with a more traditional relationship. I opted for the Amachi program and was matched with a child whose father is in prison.

Chapter 2

Meeting My Little

In 2005, I was 26 years old and just found out that I had been paired with a middle school child named Jermaine. He was 12 years old at the time and I was told that we shared a lot of interests. He was extremely athletic and loved a variety of sports. I played football and ran track through high school and continued playing basketball, soccer, and softball recreationally. He played football for his school and spent a lot of his time playing video games. We had that in common too. It would not be difficult for us to find some common ground and figure out activities to occupy our time together.

Still, there are some key differences between us. Jermaine is African-American and has a parent in prison. He is a twin being raised by his mother and grandmother. He lives in a poorer part of Nashville in government housing. The northeast Nashville area is a diverse mix of poverty and "hipster" growth. Some of Nashville's best restaurants are located in this part of town. However, it also contains the majority of all crime committed in city.

My police officer friend, Luke, told me that Nashville is divided into a pie that determines the border of each district. Each section has its own precinct, but the neighboring pieces of the pie also have precincts close to northeast Nashville's border. It is a team effort to control the crime in the area. Northeast Nashville is quite a mix of unique local businesses and deteriorating slums. Some of the revitalization efforts in the area are absolutely beautiful, but you are always close to the shoddier elements.

After work one day, I set out to meet Jermaine. I am traveling through a part of town I had never visited before and got lost. My wife and any close friend will tell you that my sense of direction is horrible and this mishap would not surprise them. I got there a little late, but I was actually given bad directions. Being late stresses me out and I was a bit anxious upon my arrival.

The house is not what I expected. Their yard was as big as mine and the house may have been a bit bigger. The neighborhood was actually a nice looking community. In fact, it looked a lot like the neighborhood where I lived in south Nashville, an area called Crieve

Hall. There was always a police car parked near Jermaine's house. I was never sure if it belonged to a resident or if it was just parked there to deter crime. However, I never felt threatened or in danger while visiting him. Only one characteristic of the community alerted me to it potentially being Section 8 housing. There were an abnormally large amount of people frequently sitting on porches and walking around the various streets. Every time I visited Jermaine, there were always lots of people milling around outside. That was peculiar to me.

I knocked on the door and entered a setting that is more in line with what I was expecting from my visit. The inside of the house was a bit dark. There were only a few lights on and the sun had begun to set. There was also a distinct smell. It was clear that the home was not cleaned regularly and that many fried meals had been cooked in the kitchen. The furniture, carpet, and décor were all dated. In addition to the 70's appliances, pictures, and carpet, there were numerous people of all ages in the house. It was an intimidating environment for a young guy like me.

After sitting down at the kitchen table, I was much more comfortable with my surroundings. I met Jermaine's mother Chastity and the BBBS counselor that would assist all of us with the match. Her name is Trish and we had a challenging relationship during her time with BBBS. Admittedly, I was about 15 minutes late to our initial meeting. However, Trish *did* give me incorrect directions to an unfamiliar part of town. This is before the GPS existed and I had to stop the car and call her to clarify where Jermaine lived.

I finally made it to the house and I apologized. Chastity was very understanding and warm. However, Trish said, "This is Adam and he will never be late again...." I laughed it off, but I admit that I was a little irritated by her comment. Still, it was not a big deal. I was excited to meet this family and find out what they expected from me. Trish and I were "friends" on Facebook for a while until we got into a small political discussion. We have very different political beliefs and our friendship would not last much longer after she left BBBS (discussing politics seems to get me "defriended" fairly regularly on Facebook). I would have several different counselors while working with Jermaine and they were all wonderful; even Trish.

At the yellow-brown kitchen table, I met Jermaine for the first time. He is a skinny, soft-spoken kid, but not shy. He seemed to like me right away and ran into his room to fetch his football trophy. It was endearing to see his enthusiasm. We sat around the table and discussed the requirements of the program and they made sure that I had phone numbers for Chastity and for Jermaine's grandmother. When asked about any other concerns that Chastity might have, she mentioned that she did not want me to expose Jermaine to any pornographic material. I was so caught off guard by that request that I am sure that I blushed. I assured her that that would not be a problem. We made plans to meet, shook hands, and I was on my way.

BBBS suggests engaging in inexpensive activities with your Little. The Big is expected to pick up the bill for each visit. Bigs are able to keep receipts and write the expenses off for taxes. However, the idea is to develop the relationship without causing a financial burden for the Big. It took me a while to understand just how little I could spend and still create a meaningful meeting, but I will elaborate later in the book.

Our first meeting was dinner and a movie. We did this regularly throughout our relationship. Jermaine would always load up on candy and some kind of slushy drink at the theater after eating his weight in food at whatever restaurant we would choose. Movies could get expensive, but I did not mind. He always had a great time at the movies and it gave me a good excuse to see an action movie or a dumb comedy (which I particularly enjoy).

That was the start of a rewarding relationship with Jermaine. We met for 6 years under the guidance of the BBBS program and tried many different activities. Throughout this book, I will share stories and concerns that surfaced during that time. However, I will start by talking to his family. I am sure that they are going to have an interesting take on the program. The following chapters will revolve around interviews that I conduct with Jermaine and his family. I want to uncover the impact that was made on each family member as well as understand their unique perspectives.

Chapter 3

Interview Day

I shared my idea to write a book with Jermaine and his family via Facebook. Their phone numbers are constantly being changed and disconnected. This was the easiest way to get the family organized. They were eager to help and I offered to buy lunch as a small bribe. I made plans to meet them in the afternoon and then take Jermaine to the movies. He requested Chinese food. His sister also asked if she could accompany us to the theater and I told her that would be fine. After some back and forth, we had finally set a date.

I had originally planned to get more authentic Chinese food from a place by my house, but I live about 25 minutes away from Jermaine. Instead of going that route, I just stopped at a place closer to his house so that the food would stay warm—Panda Express. It never ceases to amaze me how little his household experiences. They were blown away by this chain restaurant. His uncle, Aaron, asked me what was in an egg roll. What's in an egg roll?!? Jermaine's sister, Na'Licia, went back and forth on whether she should try a hot pepper that was in the kung-pow chicken. I reassured her that cooked peppers were not going to be overly hot. She abstained anyway.

I arrived about 10 minutes early. The place almost looked abandoned aside from the pit-bull chained to the side of the house. I was worried that it might not work out to do my interviews that day. I knocked to no answer and then called Jermaine. He told me that he was on his way and I waited in the car. He arrived by bike and had been at his grandmother's house the night before. He asked if I had tried to go inside and I said that nobody answered when I knocked. He went up to bang on the door and was let inside. The house was full of people. I may not have knocked loudly enough for them to hear me.

I went inside with the food and went all the way to the back room of the house. The house has an upstairs that I have never seen, but the downstairs is basically two living rooms that are separated by a kitchen. I believe that there is also one bedroom downstairs. The house is cluttered and the walls are covered by random pictures of the family. Most are school pictures, but there are a few family portraits. The living room by the front door does not look like it is used often. It has a couch, an empty aquarium, and a virtually empty entertainment center. I believe it does hold their house phone that may or may not work. The room is also dominated by an 8-foot rug with a tiger printed on it.

To get to the back living room, you must go through a small kitchen. I noticed right away that the eye of the stove was on full blast. It was a blazing red color. I thought that they may have forgotten that I was bringing lunch. However, I later figured out that they were using the stovetop as another method of heating the house. It did make the kitchen extremely warm and some of that heat did emanate to the adjoining rooms. While an effective method, it is a terrifying way to heat a home with so many children running around in it.

The back room is significantly larger than the front room. There is a television showing a cartoon—*Carmen San Diego.* They have a couple of couches around this area and in the back of the room is a long, wooden table. I would guess that it was 8 feet long and it was like a table you might find at a church or convention center. You could fold the legs to carry it. There were several chairs around it and I took a seat there. They had a space heater going in this room to keep it warm.

From here, I just took in the chaos of the house. There were about a dozen people present. Na'Licia has three kids and they are all very young. Chastity is also taking care of two other young children. Their mother is her cousin. I have not talked to Jermaine about this cousin much, but I believe that she is on drugs or incarcerated. He told me that she was unable to take care of them, but did not explain to me why. These kids, Janet and LeSean, are a little older than Na'Licia's kids. I would guess that they are in their early years of elementary school. Janet is outgoing and she was very interested in what I was doing there.

One of Na'Licia's kids was excited to show me his Spider-Man action figure. It had a magnet on its hand that allowed Spider-Man to hang from the metal trim of the table! There was a collection of five or six bikes behind the table where I was sitting, one of which was a Spider-Man bike. Jermaine's younger brother, D'Rontay, was also there, but he is a bit shy and I have only talked to him a couple of times.

Most interactions I have with Jermaine's family are educational for me. Their lives are so different from mine that I am always amazed by the way they think and relate to one another. This visit may have been the most enlightening. I came to the conclusion that everyone was sleeping when I arrived just before 1:00. There was a mad dash to get dressed and presentable. Na'Licia was actually in the laundry room asking for clothes. She had the doors pulled together with her arm sticking out so that I would not see her. The whole situation was comical.

When I sat down the food, they were extremely excited and each went to grab a plate. They all shared a single glass and talked about their respective Kool-Aid stashes. I did not see them drink anything other than the water in this one glass, but apparently they all have Kool-Aid hidden in different spots throughout the house. I did not plan to eat with them as I had a bit of a late breakfast (and could later grab something at the movies if necessary), but I was never offered a plate or any part of the meal. That was a curious observation.

At my house, we typically have a rush to get everything clean and organized when guests are expected. However, I do not think entertaining guests or dinner parties are common in Jermaine's household. I was not even offered a drink. They were not being mean or rude on purpose. In fact, they were appreciative and appeared to enjoy the exotic food. This was just another example of cultural differences for standards and etiquette. They are all extremely nice people, but live in a completely different world than the one with which I am accustomed.

As everyone finished their meals, I began to dig into my briefcase. I had pre-written a few questions for Jermaine, Chastity, Aaron, Tremaine, and Na'Licia. I had never interviewed anyone before and thought I might be nervous. I was not sure what responses my questions would get and I certainly did not want to upset or offend anyone. I will share the questions that I asked in the next several chapters as well as my impressions and interactions with Jermaine's family. There were a few questions that resulted in answers that I expected. However, there were several where their responses surprised me.

The family sat around me. AaronI had planned to interview each person more privately, but they basically formed a semi-circle in front of me. I just went with it and asked Jermaine if he would like to go first. He agreed.

Chapter 4

Jermaine

As a 20 year old, Jermaine has started to come into his own. Many people may get the impression that he is a shy young man, but he is not. He may be quiet, but I see leadership qualities in him. Jermaine understands right and wrong and he appears to be growing into the role of the head of the household. Like most ideals that I am accustomed to, this one is a bit different when studying his family. The traditional head of a household would be the father or breadwinner. He or she is responsible for the financial and moral wellbeing of the family. In Jermaine's home, this person does not exist in the traditional sense. When compared to my experience, everyone is forced to mature much more quickly in his home. They are thrust into situations at an early age that are far above their maturity level. That creates some unique results.

My stepfather, Ed, gave me an analogy before I went to college on raising kids. He explained that he treated them like a spring. If you keep the spring held tightly, it will bounce all over the place when it is freed. However, if you gently release it, it will barely move when released. Of course, the metaphor is that a child that is "gently released" will not run wild when they become adults and move out on their own. In Jermaine's case, he is basically a spring that was never really held that tightly at any point. He was exposed to sex, drugs, violence, and other adult themes before he was mature enough to handle them—at least by my standards.

How old were you when we met?
"12."
How many Big Brothers did you have? Was I your favorite?
"Just you."

I was not sure how early children could get involved with BBBS. I had assumed that he had probably worked with another Big at some point, but had never asked him about that until now. I was surprised to learn that I was his first match. We just happened to work out on the first try. Jermaine's Uncle Aaron was sitting to my left when we were talking about this. He laughed and said that Jermaine was lucky to get me. Aaron had had a few Bigs as well and none of them had worked out for him.

Do you think BBBS helped you in any way? If so, specifically tell me how.

"Yes. It helped me to see more things that I normally would not have seen. It showed me that there were other things out there. I also learned to respect more people."

This was an interesting answer. I do not know how sincere or accurate it was, but I do feel that Jermaine was doing his best to help me with my project. He is just that type of person—very respectful. I probably should have questioned him more about his last statement, but I did not. I am not sure if he was referring to white people or just people in general. Jermaine met many of my friends and family. He was always, again, very respectful to each of them. He has had dinner with my family, gone bowling with my friends, and attended sporting events with my wife. He knows just about everyone that is truly important to me. I believe he has also met a coworker or two and some of my students. I probably should have asked him to elaborate, but I did not want to force him into an awkward situation.

One of the most rewarding parts of working with the Big Brothers program was introducing Jermaine to new things. My first memory of this was when I took him to drive go-karts. He had never seen them, but was ecstatic at the thought of giving them a try. He has always been a slender person. He was never short, but I would guess he was always of average, to below-average height growing up. However, when he found out that he was not tall enough to drive the bigger cars, it did not dampen his enthusiasm. I think he also found it hilarious that I crammed myself into this mini go-kart. My knees were higher than my head when I finally settled into the vehicle. We had a blast and vowed to return when he was a couple of inches taller.

After he won our race, we had another first—Mexican food. He was 12 and had never tried it. My wife and I eat Mexican food once a week! Trying new food was an area where Jermaine was not shy. My wife and I are big foodies and love to try new restaurants. I was excited to share that interest with him. Through our many different restaurant samplings, he ate just about everything he tried. The only food I remember him disliking was sushi. Jermaine still enjoyed the experience. He got to use chopsticks for the first time, a skill that would come in handy when we went to the Japanese hibachi. He liked that a lot. We would always over-order and that would allow him to take some food home with him. He told me several times about his family eating his leftovers. As a result, he would try to hide them in the back of the refrigerator.

I would also splurge a bit for Jermaine's birthday. BBBS encourages Bigs to keep a modest budget when interacting with their Littles. However, Jermaine's birthday is in the summer and it was good opportunity to get him a few items for school. He usually was not too concerned with school clothes, but I was able to help him with his athletic endeavors. I bought him cleats several times and many other sporting goods. Unfortunately, they rarely lasted very long before they were stolen.

When I first met Jermaine at his house, he immediately showed me his football trophy. As a 12-year old, he was extremely proud of it. Sports are probably his biggest passion. He was a good athlete, but I only saw him play football one time. He played a middle school game in East Nashville. He was the back-up running back and did not play much in the first half. In the second half the starter got hurt and he ran into the game. He carried the ball twice for eighty yards and two touchdowns. It was an impressive performance. Continuing to play football became a bit much for him as he moved into high school. Jermaine would not play organized sports again.

Are you working? What are your plans for future employment?
"No. I am just relaxing and watching the kids. Sometimes I watch them here and sometimes at my granny's."

This answer was disappointing to hear, but I knew that it was likely. I talked to Jermaine a lot about college and different ways to get accepted. I was extremely blunt in many of our discussions. I explained to him that minorities can get accepted to fill certain quotas and there was nothing wrong with him taking advantage of that. He always listened to my advice, but I found it difficult to motivate him in certain areas. His family did not make higher education a priority. If he graduated from high school, then that was considered a success.

Jermaine's academic progress was one of the most eye-opening experiences I had while working with him. He actually became a fairly attentive student. Despite the low expectations around him, he carried decent grades—Bs and Cs with the occasional D. He only went to summer school one time. This was a surprisingly big achievement by his family's standards. He did graduate and I am proud of that.

When it became obvious that college was not going to happen, I shifted gears with my advice. College is not necessary to be successful in life, but I grew up thinking that it was a critical element. It was an expectation set by my parents. The only unknowns were my major and which graduate school I would attend. It was the path that I had before me and I never considered an alternative route. With Jermaine, I believed he could take a similar path. Regardless, if he could devote himself to a trade immediately after high school, that was fine alternative.

So, we talked about what he would do after high school. He found a program through his church where he could be an apprentice to an electrician. Great! Electricians make great money and are always in demand. As time moved on, this also became a bit of a pipe-dream. Jermaine kept telling me that it was still on the horizon, but it never happened. He just did not want to disappointment me. I asked him during his interview if he was still pursuing it and he finally confirmed that he was not. At this time, he stays home and watches his mother's and sister's children.

How are you doing with your Crohn's Disease?
"It's good. I still watch what I eat, but I can manage it. I go to the doctor once a month or every two weeks if I'm having a problem. I also always make sure I know where a bathroom is."

From the moment I started working with Jermaine, I knew that there was something wrong with his digestion. He would go the bathroom about once per hour. We would go to the movies and he would always need to get up sometime in the middle to find a bathroom. I am not completely sure how often he would get a check-up, but he finally went to Vanderbilt Hospital after having severe pains. They diagnosed the problem and gave him a list of foods that could trigger the pain.Now, he does a good job of watching his diet to minimize his discomfort.

This was not the case when he was originally diagnosed. He was actually hospitalized to clear some infections he was battling. Jermaine was there several days and left with a colostomy bag. He had to keep it for about three months. I went to see him in the hospital and brought him some movies to watch. I think it helped him to kill time. I later returned when it was time for him to return home. Chastity was not able to pick him up and so I took care of that. He was so happy to have the bag removed. I would have been miserable at his age to go through that.

We also went to pick up his prescriptions. It always amazes me how different grocery and convenience stores are as you move throughout the city. We went to a small pharmacy and it was extremely dirty. It was nothing like the stores on my side of town. I was ready to wait a long time to get his prescription as I knew he would use TennCare. TennCare is Tennessee's version of Medicare—medical assistance for low income families. To my surprise, we were in and out in 10 minutes. Jermaine provided his name to the pharmacist, she punched a few keys, and after a short wait, we were ready to go. It was amazing.

Jermaine is doing much better with this problem. I am sure it is the reason he is smaller in stature. However, he knows what foods trigger the problems and he is generally comfortable if there is a bathroom within reach. When he had his surgery, my boss was having a procedure about three rooms down from his. He was having colon surgery. There is quite a difference between the two on the socioeconomic scale, but only a few feet of separation for medical care.

What do you do for fun? Do you have any hobbies?

"I play basketball at the rec center and play with the dogs. The rest of the time, I'm watching the kids."

As disappointed as I have been with Jermaine's career aspirations, he is probably the most responsible person in his household. For that reason, he watches the children and makes sure that they are taken care of throughout the day. I admire his dedication to his family, but also know that it is creating a dead end for him. The longer he goes without working a steady job, the harder it will be for him to find one in the future. He will not be prepared for the grind of that routine and employers are skeptical to hire anyone that has large lapses in their work history.

His mom does not currently work, but his sister does. In theory, he could find a job right now without neglecting any of his family members. He does not have any children and that is really a blessing at this stage in his life. If Jermaine is going to rise above his situation, it would be incredibly beneficial to find some kind of employment. He recently asked to borrow a small sum of money from me (this was the first time he had ever done that) to get an apartment. I assume that it was for some sort of deposit. I declined, but suggested that he find a small job. I would even help him look, but, as a rule, I do not engage in borrowing or lending money with friends. His response was, "Thank you. I respect your rules."

Do you have a girlfriend? Do you see yourself getting married one day?

"Yes. Her name is Kicia and I can see myself getting married in a year or two."

I was blown away by that response. A year or two?! Jermaine has a serious girlfriend. This has to be the first one. He has told me about a few girlfriends here and there, but nothing was ever very serious. Honestly, I was not even sure of his impression of marriage. His grandmother has been married for quite some time. However, I know that many of his friends come from single-parent homes. Of course, he knows my wife really well and sees us interact.

I have told him on more than one occasion about the statistics and likelihood of financial success. The most difficult path is to be a single parent. The easiest path is to have two incomes with no kids. I try to tell him all about the trips and vacations that I take with my wife. My intention is not to rub it in his face or brag, but to let him know what is possible if you make good decisions and work hard. My biggest fear for him is that he gets comfortable with government assistance and does not live up to his potential.

I need to meet this girlfriend of his.

Do you have any plans to move out of your mom's house? Is there anywhere outside of Nashville that you would be interested in moving to?

"Not really. I would be interested in moving to Atlanta or Colorado, but I do not have any current plans."

One issue that I have noticed with the lower-income community is that they do not move often. It is not uncommon to see generation after generation live in similar conditions and attend the same high schools. Jermaine's family is like that. They all currently live within walking distance of each other. His mother, grandmother, sister, and uncle all went to the same two high schools. I moved several times growing up as my family changed jobs and made different economic advancements. I did not realize at the time how lucky I was. The alternative is a bit depressing.

Jermaine has been to Birmingham and Atlanta, but I believe that is the extent of his travels outside of Nashville. When he mentioned that he would like to live in Colorado, Chastity laughed at him and said, "I know why you want to live in Colorado!" The insinuation was that he wanted to move there because of the marijuana laws being loosened. He did not admit that, but she might have been right.

Marijuana use is heavy in his community. Even though I have never done a drug in my life, I am not a big proponent of drug laws. I like the idea of everyone making their own decisions about what they put into their bodies. Still, marijuana fits into the pattern of irresponsible behavior. No matter what my personal opinions may be, it is still illegal. Not only does Jermaine's family smoke together, they post pictures of what they are doing on Facebook. They certainly add some spice to my timeline.

I do not know if Jermaine will ever leave Nashville or the subsidized/project housing to which he has become accustomed. However, it cannot hurt for me to plant seeds of hope and make him dream a little bit about what is out there. It is easy to be comfortable with your current situation if you feel like nothing else is worth pursuing. If he ever feels like there is something better for him, he may find the incentive needed to build toward that goal.

Do you ever see your father?
"Yeah, I saw him in January."

He did not say anymore. I knew this would be a sensitive subject and I did not press the issue. Jermaine's father has been incarcerated since he was very young. Chastity shielded him from his father for the most part. I have asked about him three or four times and got vague responses. I usually wanted my time with Jermaine to be pleasant for him, a bit of an escape. It was okay if he did not want to talk about his father. I just wanted him to know that I would listen if he ever changed his mind about the subject.

Chastity interjected that Jermaine was going to gradually start visiting him more. She described the situation as a "work in progress." That was good to hear. It could be beneficial for him to see his father and get some advice from someone that is paying a high price for his poor decisions. It will be interesting to follow this development.

Do you see me being able to help you in the future—now that you are finished with school?
"Yeah, we can go to bars."

This was a joke, but only in part. One time, I took Jermaine to a bar. It was a dive near the bowling alley and an accident on my behalf. It was filled with smoke and older people watching football games on 15 year-old televisions. The food was terrible. However, he told me later that the sign on the door said that you had to be 21 to enter. *Whoops.* As a high school student, he loved that. He even mentioned after we started discussing this interview question. He is ready to go to a real bar now that he is approaching 21. I told him that we could do that one day, but we were not going back to that nasty place by the bowling alley.

ermaine and I will always be friends. I hope that he is still open to learning and does not give up on himself. There is only so much advice you can give. At some point he will have to want to make a change. Either way, I think he knows that I will be around and am always willing to help him. He has always been a great kid and it has been a pleasure knowing him.

Chapter 5
Na'Licia

Na'Licia is Jermaine's older sister. She is a beautiful young woman and I had never really talked with her much before this interview. From my discussions with Jermaine, Na'Licia and Chastity have had an extremely volatile relationship. That is probably true of many mothers and daughters. At times they were under the same roof, but occasionally Na'Licia lived on her own. Jermaine once told me that she had the third child because it enabled her to get her own place. My understanding of welfare laws is limited. However, I do believe that you max out your benefits after three children.

She had her first child when she was 17 and it was not long before she had a couple more. I remember one of her friends on Facebook laughing at her and saying, "Again?" the last time she posted that she was pregnant. Her response was, "I'm not trying. It just keeps happening." This is just another example of cyclical poverty. Her grandmother Charlotte had Chastity as a teenager and Chastity had Na'Licia as a teenager. Breaking the cycle is incredibly difficult.

Do you still participate in BBBS? Tell me about your Big?

"Her name is Kiana.I started working with her about the same time you started working with Jermaine. She lives in Antioch and has a bunch of foster children. We still keep in touch and go to the movies sometimes."

I have heard a few stories about Kiana through the years. Jermaine does want to travel and he has mentioned to me more than once that Kiana flew Na'Licia to Dallas. Jermaine has never flown in a plane and I think he is a bit jealous that she had that opportunity. I would like to fly him somewhere one day, but it has not happened yet. Na'Licia has worked with Kiana for quite a while and I think they have a similar relationship as Jermaine and I. My impression is that Kiana is very busy though and they probably only get together once every month or two.

Do you think BBBS had a positive influence in your life? How, specifically?

"Yes, Kiana has helped a lot. She did not help much with school, but she gave me kids' clothes. Kiana also takes me to the movies and she has given me a ride when I needed it."

There is a bit of a pattern when it comes to school work. I believe that the Big is introduced to the Little as someone that will take them out to have a good time. They are not "sold" as someone that is going to help them get their life on track. It is much easier for a child to get excited about the first possibility whereas they might balk at the second. I am sure that Kiana had the exact same hopes for Na'Licia as I did for Jermaine. Still, she was willing to help in other ways. Providing that support gives the Little some stability and someone that they can lean on when they run into problems. While this leads to positive results, they are not quite as satisfying as watching a Little find a great job or get accepted to college.

What are your kids names? How old are they and how old are you?

"Na'Dricia is five, Herman is three, and Deondros is two. I'm 22."

How did you come up with the names Na'Dricia and Deondros?

"Na'Dricia is a combination of my name and her daddy's name. His name is Bernardrick. Deondros is just a name that his daddy came up with. His name is Jalen."

A person's name and their resulting success in business and academia has been the subject of many economic studies. These studies find that the more exotic names have a harder time getting through the interview process or even getting selected for an interview. The perception may come down to racism or the belief that they will be speaking to someone foreign. However, it is still a reality. I will naturally be interested to follow the lives of these three children to see if Herman has an advantage in this area.

The name Herman was almost changed at one point. The baby was born and the name was given; a joint decision between the mother and father. However, not long after the baby was named, there was some dispute over who the father actually was. The father turned out to be another man. After some debate, the baby kept the name Herman.

Are you currently working?
"Yes, I work for Nashville Wire. I operate the machine that forms and welds oven racks. I've been there since December."

As of the time of this interview, Na'Licia had been working at this job for a month. Even with that being the case, I was pleasantly surprised to get this answer. That sounds like an incredibly stable job. She has made some decisions that have made her life more difficult. This news, however, could be an important change of course for her. If she starts to hold down a steady job, I could see this having a great lasting impact for her; and maybe for Jermaine. Sometimes when someone close to you enjoys a little success, it can spill over into your own life. I hope that is the case and I am excited for Na'Licia.

Does the government help you with rent, kids, or any other expenses?
"No, I only get food stamps."

This is a tough question to ask someone that you do not know very well, but Na'Licia is pretty blunt about things. I believed her. I do not know if that will change or if she was off of government assistance because of her new job, but this is another step in the right direction. According to WelfareInfo.org, a family of 4 can get $500 per month in food stamps and $900 per month in welfare[1]. Welfare can be used to pay for subsidized housing, heating, clothing, electricity, etc. It is means tested differently in each state.

Na'Licia is planning to move out on her own again soon. She is currently living with Chastity and that creates a fluid situation. It will be interesting to see how she continues to treat her job. Chastity should be able to watch her children while she works, but she might also see a loss in social benefits as she earns a consistent income from her employer. This is a dilemma faced by many people receiving welfare.

What do you do for fun? Do you have any hobbies?
I just work and play with my kids."

[1] "Welfare Information." US Welfare System. N.p., N.d.

Have you traveled much? Would you like to live outside of Nashville?

"I have traveled some. Kiana has taken me to Texas, Florida, Minnesota, and Michigan. I've also been to California. I have an auntie that lives in LA and I went to visit her one time. There is a lot to do there and I would like to live in California one day."

I did not realize that she had traveled so much. That was good for her. It appears that she has had a taste of what is out there and may be working toward a goal. Having three children is going to make things a little more difficult, but it is still good to see her have that interest. I could see Na'Licia having success if she really put her mind to it.

Na'Licia went to the movies with us that afternoon. She was a bit shy about the whole thing because I paid for the tickets and offered to buy concessions. At this point, Jermaine has no problem telling me what he wants. He asked for candy and popcorn and I told him that he had to pick one. That was funny. His sister quickly loosened up and ordered a drink and some candy. During the movie, Jermaine asked for some of my popcorn and I let him and Na'Licia have most of it.

We headed home after the movie ended. It had been a long afternoon and everyone was a bit tired. When I pulled in front of Chastity's house, they both exited the car. I usually thank Jermaine for hanging out with me and he also thanks me. Na'Licia was very polite as well and I think she enjoyed herself.

Chapter 6

Tremaine

Tremaine is Jermaine's twin brother.He is a handsome young man with a bright smile. The whole family has that feature in common. They all have infectious laughs and brilliant smiles. Tremaine is significantly bigger in stature than Jermaine. I noticed that about him from the moment I met him. When they were younger, he was the better athlete, but his athletic career was cut shorter than Jermaine's. He never paid much attention to his school work and trouble followed him throughout his academic career.

I picked Tremaine up a few times when I would visit Jermaine. He was always a lot of fun, but you never knew what he would do in public. We once went to a restaurant to watch football and he got a lecture from the manager about putting his feet up in the booth. I did not even notice that he was doing that. It really was not a big deal, but I had to calm Tremaine a bit so that he would not overreact. I also remember playing basketball with him at my house. He and Jermaine did not play long before they were fighting in the yard. Most of the time, his actions were good-natured, but I did notice him having a short fuse.

When I arrived at Chastity's house to conduct my interviews, I was not sure how many family members would be there. Tremaine was the only one that I requested to interview who was not there. I asked about him and Jermaine vaguely said that he was not going to make it. Chastity eventually told me that he was incarcerated. They were not clear on his exact charges or even how long he would be in jail. Jermaine said that it would depend on his rape charges. A week later, I heard that he was being released and so he must have been acquitted.

This was not Tremaine's first arrest. He was in and out of juvenile detention centers throughout his school-aged years. I remember one of his first crimes vividly. He was arrested for armed robbery. Tremaine wanted to eat pizza one day and had no money. So, he took a gun into a restaurant and robbed a worker at gunpoint for a slice of pizza. I could not believe what I was hearing when Jermaine described the incident. Tremaine's struggle with delayed gratification and self-control were causing him major problems.

Tremaine did not finish high school, but after that ship had sailed, he did show some ambition. He told me that he was going to school to be a barber. I thought that was great. That would be a solid career and something that he would do well. People naturally like Tremaine and that characteristic would suit him well when cutting hair. He even found a barber chair and it sat on their front porch for a while. Sadly, during my last visit, I caught a glimpse of that chair sitting in the corner of a room. I do not think that it has been touched in a while.

Tremaine is another tragic story of a kid that never really got going in life. He is extremely personable and likable, but makes consistently bad decisions.When I interviewed Chastity, she blamed some of Tremaine's troubles on BBBS. She mentioned that she would have liked to see them do more for him. She explained that he had tried four or five different Bigs, but none of them worked well with him. Jermaine said that one of them basically took Tremaine to the rec center that they always use to play basketball. He laughed because that was something they did anyway and did not need a Big to play basketball. Another Big was a former soldier and his style of discipline did not work at all with Tremaine.

I do hope that Tremaine finds his calling one day. He really is a pleasant young man, but you can tell immediately that there is something a little different about him.If he could get his impulses under control, I could see him doing well in life. Some kids need an iron grip around them as they mature. Unfortunately, Tremaine was given too much freedom too early and he could not handle it.

Chapter 7
Aaron

I have always liked Aaron. He has a silly sense of humor, but is maturing into a nice young man. Aaron is Jermaine's uncle. He is several years younger than Jermaine, but is Jermaine's Grandmother's son. I do not think I have ever run into a situation where someone has a younger uncle, but I have been exposed to many new things while working with Jermaine.

I first met Aaron several years ago when he requested to join Jermaine and me one day. I picked them both up and took them back to my house. Aaron asked me if I was rich. I was a little caught off-guard by his question. At the time, I was single and lived in a modest house in Bellevue, a middle class area of West Nashville. He was taken with the vaulted ceiling in the living room. That house had a bonus room with a railing that allowed you to look into the living room. I remember telling him no, but I hoped to be rich one day and that I work really hard.

We spent the day playing video games and then went to the movies. He had a great time. Aaron is also extremely personable and I believe that Jermaine is actually closer to him than he is to Tremaine. They spend a considerable amount of time together. I also think that they are good for each other. They are both good kids and can keep each other out of trouble.

Are you still in the Big Brother's program? How do you like your Big?

"I was in the program for about six months. We did not work out and I was never re-matched."

In my opinion, Aaron has the best chance of really making it out of his situation. He is driven and his mother does not allow him any slack. Until recently, he was going to a private school for high school. He is finishing his studies at the local public school. I do not believe that the change resulted from an issue with grades. His mother probably could not afford the school's tuition any longer.

Charlotte is Aaron's mother (Chastity's mother and Jermaine's grandmother) and she lives extremely close to Chastity. In fact, for a while, her house was just across the street. The house began to deteriorate and she moved a couple of blocks away from there. I found it interesting that people in subsidized housing do move occasionally. Generally, the homes are neglected. Naturally, houses will fall apart over time. When that happens, the government steps in to renovate and moves the occupants to another house.

Charlotte seems to be close to Chastity, but she has clearly taken a special interest in Aaron. He has been on a tight leash as long as I have known him. His private school makes their core mission obvious. They are committed to doing whatever it takes to have a 100% graduation rate and to send each student to a four-year college.

How old are you now? Are you planning to go to college?
"I am 18 and I do plan to go to college. I have looked at TSU (Tennessee State University), Austin Peay, MTSU (Middle Tennessee State University), and WKU (Western Kentucky University)."

Going to college would be a major accomplishment. Not only would Aaron see personal rewards from this achievement, but he would lay the groundwork for future generations to go to college. This metamorphosis is something that I will explore in more detail later in the book. Small changes and achievements can have monumental ripple effects for a family's future.

The schools that Aaron is considering are all fairly local. TSU is just minutes away from his house. It is a historically black school, but would be a great choice for him and very convenient. Austin Peay is located in Clarksville, TN and it is northwest of Nashville, near the Kentucky border. It is a growing school and would be another excellent choice. MTSU has become the biggest school in the state and it is southeast of Nashville, in Murfreesboro, TN. Western Kentucky is not far away and offers in-state tuition to students coming from many counties in Middle Tennessee. Aaron would flourish at any of these public institutions.

What are you going to study? How are your grades now?
"I don't really know what I'll study. Music maybe. I'm learning piano and guitar in school right now. My last report card was all As and B. I occasionally have Cs."

This was great to hear. I had always assumed that Aaron was a good student. I knew that Charlotte "cracked the whip" when it came to his schoolwork to keep him in line. His academy was strict with its academic standards and he was always working harder than his other school-aged family members. MTSU is actually one of the premier music schools in the country. It would be the most difficult program for him to be admitted.

I remember entering college and not completely knowing what I would do either. When my parents asked me, I mentioned teaching to them. That notion was immediately vetoed because it would create a financial struggle for me. I was a reasonable person and accepted that argument. Little did I know, I would work a banking job, but also follow my passion and teach college students. I wonder what my parents would have said to me if I had told them I was going to study music in college.

For Aaron, things are a little different. I am glad that he has a motivation for going to school. Still, the music business is a tough field. I am fairly familiar with it because Belmont University (where I teach) also has an excellent music business major. It is extremely competitive, but still does not guarantee a lucrative job after graduation. My thought on the matter is that Aaron will do well if he follows through with his college aspirations—*period.* Once he gets into school, I might have a talk with him about the practicality of his decision.

Do you have a girlfriend? Do you see yourself getting married one day?

"No, I don't have a girlfriend. I do see myself getting married, but not until after college."

This is another solid answer. If Aaron is able to wait for a relationship, it will be easier for him to navigate college. It will also give him the opportunity to continue to mature before he makes a decision about the type of person he wants to marry. As I mentioned before, Aaron's mother has been married for quite some time and so he has been exposed to a successful marriage. Marrying the right person is major factor in a person's overall happiness in life. Delaying that decision is an important component in making a lasting choice.

Where would you like to live when you get out of school?

"Outside Nashville. I would like to live in California. I have always dreamed of visiting Japan though."

I asked him to go further with his interest in Japan, but he did not have anything concrete to mention. That was an interesting choice though. We are seeing more Eastern influence on the West over time. Many cartoons and other products are developing in Asian countries before gaining interest in the United States. My generation is more accustomed to the exact opposite situation. However, times are changing and we no longer have a monopoly on cultural influence.

What hobbies do you have? What do you like to do with your free time?
"I hang out with my friends and play video games. I also like to play the keyboard."

He is still a kid and is still learning new interests. Of course, I am twice his age and still play video games. I will probably never stop. Aaron made his music interest clear. Music is a great hobby and many studies have shown how closely it relates to mathematics and other academic disciplines. Learning music has many benefits and has been shown to be extraordinarily helpful for students.

Is there anything I can do to help you?
"If you could find me a cheap keyboard, that would be great."

I laughed at this answer. I told him that I would keep my eyes open for a cheap keyboard, but that was not my intent with the question. As he moves closer to college, I thought he might need some direction. I mentioned to him that I would also be happy to help him with any college concerns he might have. Aaron was a little embarrassed, but he said that he could use help there as well. I do not think there are any college graduates in his family. Just being admitted to a school would be an amazing accomplishment.

I will continue to monitor Aaron's maturation with great interest. He has a real shot at making something of himself and derailing the cyclical poverty of his family. He appears to have the drive as well as the support of his parents. This is a critical combination for a child to reach their full potential. I suspect that Charlotte made a commitment to him when he was young. It could have been a reaction to seeing her other children struggling with life and making critical errors as young adults.

I do not know her other son very well. His name is Andre and he lives with his girlfriend and has a child or two. He does seem to hold a regular job. However, he also painted himself into a corner by having a child at an early age. I also recall Andre taking Jermaine to get tattoos when he turned 16. Jermaine now has "North" printed down one forearm and "Side" printed down the other one. This is a tribute to the northern part of Nashville where they live. I did not ask Chastity about her thoughts on that, but my parents would have lost their minds.

Aaron is clearly the "golden child" of the family. In my opinion, he is held to a different set of standards. He is expected to do his school work and he is the closest person I can find in his family to being held accountable to the same standards my parents set for me. I offered to take Aaron with us when we went to the movies and he had to call his mom to check if it would be ok. I found out that Charlotte requires him to volunteer at a senior center each Saturday. He called and said, "I can't go to the movies, can I?" She, of course, said "no." I will need to work with him on his salesmanship.

Like the rest of his family, Aaron is a genuinely likeable person. I am friends with him on Facebook and crack up at his "selfies." He likes to post pictures of himself in different poses and to show-off his abs. He has a great outlook and excellent sense of humor. I do hope that his parents continue to push him and that he reaches his goals. He has worked hard and it would be wonderful to see him rewarded for his efforts.

Chapter 8
Chastity

Chastity is Jermaine's mom and I honestly do not know her very well.I have chatted with her casually through the years while picking him up at the house. Still, I would not say that I have had any in-depth talks with her (without counting this interview). It is an interesting observation for me because my parents were so involved in my life. They knew everyone that I ever spent any quality time with while growing up. I am sure that Jermaine would fill her in on our visits and she would also talk to our case manager with BBBS. So, it is possible that her concerns were satisfied between the two.

While Jermaine was in high school, I was required to fill out the occasional survey on his development as well as check in with our case worker each quarter. That person changed fairly frequently (every other year or so), but each was diligent in her work. I would answer basic questions on how often we were meeting and what we were doing. I would also express my concerns. Chastity was basically asked the same questions. I do not recall ever having any complaints or suggestions from her. I am glad that she trusts me, but I would have been happy to sit down with her if she felt that certain areas needed special attention.

Chastity is not much older than me. She also had children very young and already has several grandchildren. The thought of being in her position terrifies me, but it is common in her community. She is close to her children, but I feel that they see her as more of a friend than a parent. This was one of my more intriguing interviews. I was truly curious to know what Chastity though about the BBBS program.

Did you have a Big Sister when you were younger? If not, how did you hear about the program?

"I never had one when I was younger. I heard about the program because the school suggested that I look into it for Tremaine."

That made a lot of sense. Tremaine has struggled with discipline and authority for as long as I have known him. I am sure that his teachers picked up on that right away and reached out to Chastity with suggestions that might help him. She mentioned that a child needs to be 10 years old before they are eligible for the program. In my opinion, that is a little late. It would be much better to start at an earlier age and I will further examine that topic later in the book.

Are you able to get any government assistance?
"I do get some help."

Chastity was not as blunt as Na'Licia when talking about government assistance.She was sitting with her family around her and I did not want to push the issue. Had we been in more private setting, I may have asked for some details. I imagine that she does get a decent amount of welfare assistance because of the children in her home.

Do you have a boyfriend? Do you ever plan to get married?
"No, I don't have a boyfriend. I could see myself getting married one day. They say that love will find you when you're not looking for it."

I have asked Jermaine from time-to-time if his mom was dating anyone.Having an adult male in his life would be quite a change for him. Jermaine usually told me that she did not. However, one of her boyfriends made the news.

Chastity was dating a known gang member. He was a Crip. I will talk more about gangs in Nashville later, but this is a relatively infamous group. The fate of many gang members generally comes down to prison or death. Chastity's boyfriend suffered from the former. He was incarcerated.

When imprisoned, he did leave a few odds and ends with Chastity. The most notable object was his vehicle that was a known gang car. Chastity decided to drive around the SUV while he was in jail. This was a critical mistake as a rival gang, the Bloods, opened fire on the car. Chastity was hit once and Tremaine was hit three times. Several of his wounds were very close to his spine and vital organs. Miraculously, he made a full recovery. Chastity and her family were extremely lucky to survive a poor decision on her part.

How many people are living in your home?
"Six or seven."

Chastity definitely has a crowded house at the moment. Janet, DaVon, Jermaine, Na'Licia, D'Rontay, Herman, Na'Dricia, and Deondros are all under one roof. Including Chastity, that makes nine people. They also have three pit-bulls. I started to run though the different people that lived there with her and she laughed. It was as if she was not completely sure who was there. Chastity seemed a little "off" during our interview. I was not sure if she was high, nervous, or acting odd because she had just awoken.

Are you currently working?
"No. I know that I need to find a job though. I can't depend on the government forever. My dream has always been to open a daycare with my mom."

Charlotte has run a daycare of some sort as long as I have known Jermaine. There were always plenty of kids to watch from the neighborhood and from her own family. It is an easy business to start. She has a stable home and the people in her community can trust her. It is also very easy to undercut the typical prices of a licensed daycare.

Chastity has had employment here and there. I remember one such job she had at a local grocery store. It did not last long. Jermaine told me that she was being "disrespected" by her boss and quit. Other attempts to work have had similar outcomes for her.

Have you ever considered moving away from Nashville?
"I am born and raised here. I would consider moving somewhere else though."

She did not have any details or specific places in mind. This came across as more of an abstract thought.

Do you think Big Brothers Big Sisters has helped your children? How so?
"I think it has been helpful. I wish that it would have helped Tremaine more. It has given them a way to experience things that I couldn't provide. It has broadened their horizons and given them another person to talk to."

To my earlier point, I am not completely sure about what objective Chastity actually had for the program. Her participation comes across as a bit of a "Hail Mary" from a desperate parent. She was hoping that exposing her children to solid role-models would have a positive impact in their lives. It was an excellent gesture on her part, but concrete goals between a mother and the Big would have been more impactful. Of course, I did not completely understand that until much later in the process.

Do you ever interact with Jermaine's father?
"No, I haven't seen him in a while. Jermaine saw him after Christmas though."

Jermaine never talks about his father and so I thought I might get some information about him from Chastity. She was just as tight-lipped on the subject. I will continue to follow Jermaine's relationship with him. I do hope that he continues to visit. However, I do get the feeling that Chastity is not interested in him any longer.

Have you ever been arrested?
I had this question written to ask her, but could not pull the trigger. Her children were around her and it would not have been appropriate. This interview was difficult anyway. I may not have asked her this question even if we were talking one-on-one.

What advice would you have for your children as they grow into adulthood?
"I am still learning myself. I would say to try new things and explore."

Chastity struggled with this question. She groaned and laughed while she tried to come up with an answer. She told me that it was a tough question and I laughed with her and told her that "the mom gets the harder questions." She finally came up with the answer I listed above, but I had to help her a bit. After several minutes of working through it, I let her off the hook. When I wrote this item into my agenda for her, I never thought it would be so challenging.

Chastity genuinely loves her family. She is a young woman that became a mother far too early in her life (and then subsequently became a grandmother). She has always been kind and gracious to me and I feel like she is doing her best given her difficult situation. Still, Chastity is proof that good intentions are really not enough to escape a generational cycle of poverty. Someone along the line must make better decisions and avoid the temptations that constantly surround them.

Before long, most of Chastity's children will be adults. She could theoretically re-enter the workforce. I fear that she will have gone so long without consistent employment that it will doom her chances to work in the future. She will be competing for jobs with younger people with a similar skillset. Chastity may find it impossible to really change anything about her situation at this point.

As we proceed through this book, there will be a reoccurring theme about avoiding cyclical poverty and breaking that cycle. I will examine schools, language, food, politics, clothing and other issues that continue to create persisting challenges to impoverished families. It will be important to dissect the differences in culture to find the culprits that keep causing this issue generation after generation. Once pinpointed, we will begin to discuss possible solutions.

Part II

Defining a Culture

Chapter 9

Speaking the Same Language

Jermaine and I have never had any problems communicating. He speaks fairly well and I talk to him as I would anyone else. However, I have noticed that he speaks differently around his family and friends. I really picked up on that difference when I first picked up Jermaine with Tremaine. It was almost as if they spoke a different language. Interestingly enough, I remember my parents saying that I did that with my friends. They could barely understand what we were saying to each other.

So, why is there a difference in speech while speaking to someone within your family (or that you are more comfortable with) versus someone that might call for a more formal version of your language? This would appear to be a natural phenomenon. For our purposes, the key to examining it is to determine if there is a cultural difference. A culture is closely defined by its language, food, politics, and clothing. Is there an established difference between the culture of the consistently poor and the culture of the consistently wealthy? Or, is this a less complicated matter where people simply use a less formal dialect when conversing with equals?

If you watch much television, it will not take you long to find a show on The Learning Channel or Discovery Channel that makes a spectacle of a low-income family conducting their everyday lives. They might be parading their daughters in a pageant, making moonshine, or engaging in some other activity that is foreign to most of the population. The more entertaining "characters" are only modestly educated and carry a thick regional accent and virtually unintelligible dialect. Some speak so poorly that the station will actually include captioning. They are captioning someone speaking English!

Nevertheless, it is evident that the people communicate clearly with each other. For this reason, it is possible to believe that the communication gap is cultural. They might as well speak a different language from the viewing audience in some instances, but their dialect works with those that live in the region. Is there a difference in speech between the rich and poor so significant that it keeps the members of each class immobile? The concept is that the rich speak as though they are rich and the poor speak as though they are poor. Rich people are comfortable speaking with others that "sound rich" just as poor people prefer to converse with others that "sound poor."It is difficult to avoid realizing the truth in this idea.

In 1996 this difference in speech came to the national forefront because of a California school board decision. Geoffrey K. Pullum wrote a paper on the subject titled *African American Vernacular English Is Not Standard English With Mistakes*[1]. He refers to a *New York Times* editorial which explains that Oakland had "declared that black slang is a distinct language." Pullum points out that Oakland is a poor community on the east side of the San Francisco Bay and half of its population is African-American.

The author contradicts the *New York Times* article and insists that African American Vernacular English (AAVE) is definitely not "slang." However, the national perception of this idea was certainly mixed. AAVE was seen as "street talk" or a vernacular of the lower classes. There was public outcry about moving away from proper English and it became a mainstream issue for talk-radio. Pullum further explains that there are distinct differences between slang and an actual language. Slang is more of a "parasite on some larger and more encompassing host language."

The more common name for AAVE is *Ebonics.* Mr. Pullum explains that the term came from a combination of the words *Ebony* and *Phonics.* Using this term did not help the cause of creating legitimacy for AAVE being an actual language or dialect. The term was highly ridiculed and the butt of several jokes for the next year. Still, the author explains that AAVE is much more than just slang terms and grammatical errors.

The author uses Standard English as his example. Pullum offers several instances where different phrases and spellings are used for each dialect of the same language of English. Brits and Americans say "herb" differently. Brits pronounce the "h" and Americans do not. Brits add a "u" to some words; *honour* for example. I am currently reading a book by a British author named Martin Jacques. He uses the term "per cent" rather than "percent" in his writing. I was unaware of that difference and thought that I had caught a typo.

[1] Pullum, Geoffrey K. "African American Vernacular English Is Not Standard English with Mistakes." Geoffrey Pullum Ebonics Article in Nature:03-31-97. Nature Magazine, 31 Mar. 1997. Web. 27 Mar. 1997.

This article regarding AAVE makes some compelling arguments for the consideration of *Ebonics* as a dialect of English. It has the properties of many other languages throughout the world and it certainly has some common traits that a dialect might have. Pullum's main point is that using a vernacular that is common to an area can help you to communicate more clearly with its people. Naturally, it is also instrumental in teaching. It simply makes sense to incorporate the regional dialect when you are presenting new information to students.

Legitimate or not, does it make sense to encourage a different dialect among the black community? Just before the idea of using Ebonics surfaced in Oakland, Felicia Lee wrote an article for the *New York Times*[2]. She stated that linguists were noticing the growth of AAVE within poor, urban communities. Lee has a different take on the appeal of the alternate language:

> Standard English "The persistence of the dialect reflects, in part, the growing resistance of some black young people to assimilate and their efforts to use language as part of a value system that prizes cultural distinction. It also stems from the increasing isolation of black inner-city residents from both whites and middle-class blacks, and stems as well from a deep cynicism about the payoffs of conforming."

The article then discusses the worry that many educators display about the youth in lower-income areas learning proper English at all. As we will discuss in chapter 16, there is an inherent stigma with some black people portraying themselves as "white." Speaking Standard English fits into this category. Classmates expect their peers to speak with the AAVE dialect or they are seen as an "Uncle Tom."

This controversial topic is one to be handled carefully by the English teachers of this country. Not allowing students to use Ebonics has been considered racist and has caused backlash from several communities. With children poking fun of other children and school boards having ambiguous policies on the subject, it is challenging to teach Standard English. Teachers have mixed feelings on

[2] Lee, Felicia R. "Lingering Conflict in the Schools: Black Dialect vs. Standard Speech." The New York Times. The New York Times, 04 Jan. 1994.

the subject. While some see AAVE as a way to connect with their students, others feel that they are not providing them a necessary tool for the business world.

One interesting point shared by Lee and Pullum is the idea of dialect switching. Does a person have the ability to switch back and forth between Ebonics and Standard English? Some feel that a person should not have to make the switch. They say that it is a racist notion. Still, it is clear that knowing Standard English is an important skill for a student trying to enter the business world. Racist or not, he or she will not be able to use Ebonics in a job interview.

This idea seems to be a reasonable compromise by the academic community. It is becoming more acceptable to use AAVE among friends, family, and even in the classroom.However, in more formal settings, students should switch to Standard English. For example, casual interactions between students and teachers could use either dialect, but an actual presentation would be offered using Standard English. It is not uncommon for anyone (at any point along the socioeconomic ladder) to use this type of policy. Almost everyone is more proper in a formal setting and relaxes in a casual setting.

The crucial idea in this discussion is the division that takes place between the more impoverished areas and the wealthier areas. To Mr. Pullum's point, there is certainly nothing wrong with speaking another language or dialect. We do it when we visit other English-speaking countries and we do not expect them to speak our version of English so that we feel more comfortable.

Nevertheless, there are several key ways that Ebonics fails to meet the benchmark of being a language or dialect. The most obvious is the reception that an outsider might get when trying to use the dialect. Some countries may be a bit snobbish about their native language (not pointing fingers), but they are generally appreciative of your efforts to speak in that tongue. This is not true with AAVE—*at all.* If someone that regularly speaks Standard English attempts to speak Ebonics to someone that speaks that dialect regularly, it can turn into quite a spectacle. The best case scenario is that everyone involved laughs and ridicules the effort. However, there is also the chance that the person preferring Ebonics is deeply offended.

For that reason, AAVE struggles to pass the language litmus test. The prevailing characteristic of the dialect is that it is used as a means of classification and separation. Others are not welcome to speak the language of Ebonics unless they hit a certain qualifier.To that end, AAVE is also keeping a wider separation between socioeconomic classes. Rich and educated people know how other rich and educated people sound and they look for that quality in their speech when hiring.

In 2004, comedian Bill Cosby gave a speech at an NAACP event to commemorate the 50th anniversary of *Brown vs. Board of Education.* Cosby has a doctorate in education and took this opportunity to comment on the monumental court decision that ended segregation in schools. Here is an excerpt from his speech which is commonly called, *We Can't Blame White People*[3]:

> "Brown versus the Board of Education is no longer the white person's problem. We've got to take the neighborhood back. We've got to go in there. Just forget telling your child to go to the Peace Corps. It's right around the corner. It's standing on the corner. It can't speak English. It doesn't want to speak English. I can't even talk the way these people talk: "Why you ain't where you is go ra?" I don't know who these people are. And I blamed the kid until I heard the mother talk. Then I heard the father talk. This is all in the house. You used to talk a certain way on the corner and you got into the house and switched to English. Everybody knows it's important to speak English except these knuckleheads. You can't land a plane with, "Why you ain't..." You can't be a doctor with that kind of crap coming out of your mouth. There is no Bible that has that kind of language. Where did these people get the idea that they're moving ahead on this. Well, they know they're not; they're just hanging out in the same place, five or six generations sitting in the projects when you're just supposed to stay there long enough to get a job and move out."

> "Now, look, I'm telling you. It's not what they're doing to us. It's what we're not doing. 50 percent drop out. Look, we're raising our own ingrown immigrants. These people are fighting hard to be ignorant. There's no English being spoken, and they're walking and they're angry. Oh God, they're angry and they have pistols and they shoot and they do stupid things. And after they kill somebody, they don't have a plan. Just murder somebody. Boom. Over what? A pizza? And then run to the poor cousin's house."

---

[3]Cosby, Bill. "We Can't Blame White People." Snopes.com: Bill Cosby on Blaming White People. N.p., N.d. Web. 17 May 2004.

Dr. Cosby and his wife Camille are extremely successful African-Americans. They are incredibly philanthropic and are passionate about the advancement of black people. Dr. Cosby truly cares enough to stand in front of a crowd that will have mixed emotions about his spoken words. He is probably considered an Uncle Tom by some, but his message is clear—and spot on accurate. Black people need to stop worrying about common behaviors they might share with white people.

I am not going to tell you that white people are squeaky clean. Racism does exist and there are many white people that do want to prevent black people from being successful. However, the battle that looms between races hurts black people much more than it hurts white people. When the African-American community focuses on "keeping it real", they are only hurting their chances for success. Speaking a language that prevents one from having a job may garner respect from others in the community, but it certainly has no detrimental impact on the white community.

In fact, this modus operandi only benefits people of other races. Denise E. Troutman and Julia S. Falk wrote a passage in *The Journal of Negro Education* entitled *Speaking Black English and Reading—Is there a Problem of Interference?*[4]? They mention that "National surveys report that black children score significantly lower on reading achievement tests than do their white peers of the same socioeconomic and residential status." They continue by commenting that, "there are a disproportionate number of black children in remedial reading classes." Being unreceptive to successful stepping stones is crippling the black community.

UC Berkley linguist, John McWhorter, is concerned with the non-receptive nature that many in the African-American community exhibit toward education[5]. McWhorter has no problem with the casual use of AAVE or even using it in the classroom. However, he does not want Black English to be taken too far or become a standard. His main reasons are:

[4]Troutman, Denise E., and Julia S. Falk. "Speaking Black English and Reading–Is There a Problem of Interference?" The Journal of Negro Education Vol 51(2), N.d. Web. 1982.

[5]McWhorter, John. "Authentically Black: Essays for the Black Silent Majority Hardcover – January 27, 2003." Authentically Black: Essays for the Black Silent Majority: John McWhorter: 9781592400010: Amazon.com: Books. Gotham, N.d. Web. 7 Jan. 2003.

1. Because translation between these close dialects is not the problem, doing this would be like trying to put out a house fire with an eyedropper. Sure, it might do some tiny, insignificant good here and there *but while it was doing this*—
2. It would make black kids look stupid, as if they were incapable of making the two-inch jump between such close dialects while kids in Brooklyn, Appalachia and white Mississippi do it without comment (or – if they fail in school, dialect is not thought to be the reason).

My fear relates more to McWhorter's second point. Speaking in Ebonics can make a person look stupid. It scares employers (especially white ones) and it makes it easier for an interviewer to bypass a viable black candidate. For African-Americans, or anyone that speaks a unique regional dialect that presents a challenge for the Standard English speaker, it is important to be able to shift gears depending on the situation. A person that can only speak regional diction without the ability to use Standard English is like a boxer that only has one punch. The jab is the punch that wins fights and it turns a brawler into a true boxer. Swinging wildly only works in certain situations. You have to learn the jab if you want to be successful.

If a black person is able to learn Standard English and use it in the correct setting, it probably does not matter that that they use AAVE in their personal lives. However, the difference between the two versions of the same language continues to grow. I certainly use a different vernacular when talking with my friends and family than I do when conversing with clients, teaching class, or giving a speech—but it is not *that* different. Moving from one extreme to the other within the same language presents unique challenges.

William Raspberry wrote an article that can be found on Philly.com entitled *'Black English' Vs. 'Standard English': How Can Schools Deftly Do The Right Thing*[6]? He refers to the switching between dialects as "code-switching." Raspberry states the importance of knowing a formal style,but the difficulty that teachers have implementing Standard English. That idea can easily be construed as racially insensitive. For that reason and because the two versions of English are so different, many of our young boxers are only equipped with the haymaker style when they leave school. Raspberry beautifully explains that, "Good English, well spoken and well written, will open more doors than a college degree. Bad English will slam doors that you didn't even know existed."

[6]Raspberry, William. "'Black English' Vs. 'Standard English': How Can Schools Deftly Do The Right Thing?" Philly.com. N.p., 06 Feb. 1991.

In Jermaine's family, I could see Aaron having the ability to code switch. He can speak one way with his family and friends, but another way around authority figures (including his mother). I have talked to Aaron quite a bit and can verify the he speaks Standard English well. Still, you might be surprised to see some of his less formal communication. Here are some excerpts I found on his Facebook page:

> "Why are people so damn ignorant now-uh-days? If someone crosses your mind, at least hit em' up. That whole "I'm not texting unless THIS person text first" thing is STUPID
>
> Fuck Those Who Don't Fuck Witcha ! Just Stay True To You And What You Do
>
> Fuck it, I don't even tint it, they should know who's in it."

Here are some posts from Chastity:

> "So y'all think its a game Na'Licia and ThaOneandonly Ms'Kim....them dicks gone be waiting on y'all when u pull up.......BELIEVE ME..... Y'ALL SOME T.H.O.T.S
>
> Time to celebrate. ...#fireinthahole (this was a caption next to a picture of her smoking marijuana)
>
> WTF......is Miami doin liking like sum f ucking 2yrs old out there..... 18 to 43.......end of 1st. quarter...tha wizards gettin in that ass.....#teammia"

Na'Licia:

> "If A Nigga Think He Gone Treat Me Like An OPTION . I Need A Calculator So I Can Tell Him HOW Many Times He Got Me Fucked Up !
>
> Real Niggas Take Care Of They Kids No Matter Wat If A Bitch Say It's Me Or Yo Kids A Real Nigga Gone Say Bye My Kids Gone Always Be Hea You Jus Part Time You Can Leave Me Wen U Want My Kids My Life A Real Nigga Will Do Wat He Gotta Do Fa His Kids Before He Get His Bitch Right"

Jermaine does not post often on Facebook, but here are a couple of his:

> "my granny was like who fuck up my toilet seat... nigga be like it wasn't me (next to a picture of a toilet seat that was laying on the ground next to the toilet)
>
> what! that real, that deep,that burning, that amazing unconditional, insepar love..
>
> these niggas tryna eat my snacks!!"

I know that Facebook posts can be taken with a grain of salt. You can probably find similar posts from kids in the most affluent white communities as well. However, it is curious to see Chastity's posts intermingled within the posts of her children. I am also "friends" with my parents on Facebook. That causes me to reconsider what I post to some degree. With Jermaine's family, it simply flows back and forth as if they were simply friends. The formality that a child might have with a parent does not exist.

As I matured, I was given more slack by my parents on the way I acted. I could relax my grammar to some extent and occasionally cuss in front of my parents without things getting awkward. However, I still feel that need to be respectful and proper around most adults. You would not catch me using slang around someone older than myself. I know that many people are raised the same way.In Jermaine's home, they are less formal with everyone. They do not carry the same need for Standard English and it is never really learned properly.

I once played Scrabble with Jermaine. I honestly do not know what I was thinking with this idea, but he was always a good sport when I suggested something new. Until that day, I did not truly understand the depth of this language problem. His spelling was poor and he could not put together a word that contained more than one syllable. I felt badly about the situation and it was never my intent to humiliate him. So, I started to help him with his words as we completed the game.

I remember playing Scrabble and other educational games often as a child. It was common within my family and even among my friends. I could not believe how difficult it would be for Jermaine to participate. He was uncomfortable and was basically just waiting for the game to finish. My wife and I still talk about that game to this day. It was a learning moment for us. I began to realize just how unrealistic my expectations were for him.

It is certainly possible to speak Ebonics and switch to Standard English when the time comes. Still, there is some doubt as to the practicality of that notion. If someone is raised speaking a more rural or urban dialect, then they are less likely to be taught Standard English and are certainly less receptive to it. When you combine that issue with the focus that the African-American culture has on being different from those that speak Standard English, you can see the problem that has developed.

Using Standard English in the written and spoken form is a requirement for education and business. The urban community could take a big step forward by embracing that fact. As mentioned by the theme of Dr. Cosby's speech, they are only hurting themselves by insisting on using a completely different language. Their actions are not hurting white people in the least, but are having a drastically detrimental effect on African-Americans. The language barrier is not only separating the races, but it is preventing the black community from seeing consistent advancement.

Chapter 10

Soul Food

I do love Southern cuisine. It is the true comfort food of this country. It is high in fat, calories, cholesterol, and every other negative category that can be attributed to the dining experience. In the South, it is not hard to find regional cuisine. Any restaurant labeled as a "meat-n-three" will provide what you are looking for in this arena. From a cultural perspective, the South is unmistakable in their cuisine. It is incorporated into every activity and it spans the entire socioeconomic ladder. I have had the classic Southern dish, shrimp and grits in a dive and I have had it at some of the finest restaurants in Nashville.

According to a CalorieLab.com 2011 study, Mississippi and Alabama are the fattest states in the Union[1]. Tennessee, Louisiana, Kentucky, and South Carolina are all in the top 10. The Southern culture is defined by food. Even within the South, there are subsets of cultural differences when examining its unique cuisines. You can find the spicier Cajun cooking in Louisiana and Mississippi as well as different seafood dishes that are native to the Gulf and Atlantic coasts. When the earlier settlers were introduced to the new land, Southerners started to learn what would grow in different areas. From that point, it was full speed ahead and we rarely miss an opportunity to eat in this part of the country.

Within the Southern diet is a strong African influence. Beth McKibben of *Deep South Magazine* conducted an interview with Atlanta chef Todd Richards on the subject[2]. He explained that African slaves cooked, not to shape cuisine, but for survival:

> "You have to look at two things: what came with the slaves on the boat and what they had to work with when they got to America. There was a strong Native American influence in the early beginnings of Southern food when slaves began arriving: crops like corn and techniques

[1] "Mississippi Is the Fattest State for 6th Straight Year, Colorado Still Leanest, Rhode Island Getting Fatter, Alaska Slimmer." CalorieLab, N.d. Web. 30 June 2011.

[2] McKibben, Beth. "The Real Roots of Southern Cuisine | Deep South Magazine – Southern Food, Travel & Lit." The Real Roots of Southern Cuisine. Deep South Magazine, N.d. Web. 3 Dec. 2012.

> like frying. Then, you have crops and techniques that came over from West Africa with the slaves, like the peanut (or goober peas), okra (or gumbo) and stewing techniques. There's also daily survival ingredients like watermelons, which served as canteens in the fields. It's 95 percent water. The slaves also used the rind as soles for their shoes. So ingredients like this that are now part of Americana and the Native American influence really started shaping Southern food very early on. But you can't discount other influences like that of the Spanish and Portuguese through Louisiana or the Latin influence through parts of Texas. The slaves worked with what was available to them and adapted their daily diets accordingly."

Richards explains that Southern cuisine is a combination of African staples with the preservation methods that were introduced by the Native Americans. The slaves found that the native vegetables of Africa grew well in the South and they could be combined with the salted meats that were new to them. This is the origination of the Southern dish and the meat-n-three. He continues by explaining that one-pot cooking started with slaves. Gumbo and cornbread were easy to make and relatively quick for that reason.

Chef Richards is a wealth of information on the subject. He also pointed out that salted meats would preserve other items if they were stored underneath the meat. Normally, this spot was reserved for greens. Greens were also flavored by this method. When the greens were eaten, then the meat could be fried. Frying is actually not a method invented in the South. It was a technique concocted by the Native Americans, but borrowed by the slaves. Africans were not accustomed to preparing meat and learned quite a bit about it from the American-Indians. In fact, Richards pointed out that Lewis and Clark were taught to fry meat as well as turn it into jerky during their travels.

The perseverance and resourcefulness of African-Americans through slavery is quite amazing. Many were given horrible conditions and their allocations of food were generally the parts of the animal that were discarded by their white masters. As you may expect, these food items are not healthy and may have led to some longer-term generational problems as well.

Matthew Bigg of *Reuters* wrote an article on the subject entitled

Bad diet ups cancer risk for poor, black women[3]. Here are the specifics of this research:

> "The study of more than 150 women living in public housing in Washington, D.C., found that 61 percent of them met none or just one of five goals for maintaining a healthy diet.
>
> The goals included adequate consumption of fruit and vegetables, a low percentage of fat intake, consuming no alcohol, eating moderate calories and adhering to a U.S. government Healthy Eating Index, which measures overall quality of diet."

He continues by revealing that only about one percent of women in this study hit all six categories. There were some other correlations made as well. Younger women were more likely to eat fast food than older women. Bigg believes that there are "structural factors in society" that are working against these low-income families. Many lack the knowledge and skill to make a healthy meal. This is a real problem because there is also a link between depression and smoking to a poor diet.

The causation and correlation between diet, access to food, and general preference among more impoverished communities is debatable. Like the chicken and the egg, the basic debate comes down to one idea: Are poorer communities eating an unhealthy diet because only unhealthy foods are sold in these areas? Or, do poorer communities prefer unhealthy foods and the laws of supply and demand are at work?

The answer may lie somewhere in the middle.Emily Alpert Reyes wrote an article entitled *Poor, mostly black areas face supermarket 'double jeopardy'* for *The Los Angeles Times* that sheds some light on the issue[4]. She took a look at the problem that poorer communities face when trying to access healthy foods. There are simply more convenience stores than actual grocery stores in low-income communities. The general idea is that convenience stores carry more foods that are high in salt, sugar, and fat while you can find ample produce and healthier choices in a large grocery store.

[3] subject

[4] women

The author references a study conducted by Johns Hopkins University where poor, black neighborhoods face a "double disadvantage." These neighborhoods have less grocery stores than wealthy, white neighborhoods, but they also have less grocers than poor, white neighborhoods. There is a clear racial difference in this allotment.

Even with that said, all of the blame cannot be attributed to simply needing a better concentration of grocery stores in poorer, African-American parts of town. Poor, Latino areas were found to have a higher number of grocers than black communities with a comparable income. Latinos generally have better diets and have a higher demand for better food at every point along their demographic's socioeconomic ladder.

The research pointed out that a nationwide program to promote better eating habits probably was not necessary. This education initiative should be targeted at areas that routinely have poor diets. M. Cristina F. Garces and Lisa A. Sutherland have an article on Diet.com titled African-American *diet*[5]. In the year 2000, 70% of African-Americans were overweight according to their BMI and 40% were obese. The authors mention that there are some valuable foods in their typical diet like "greens, yellow vegetables, legumes, beans, and rice." They also point out that, "Because of cooking methods and the consumption of meats and baked goods, however, the diet is also typically high in fat and low in fiber, calcium, and potassium.... African Americans experience high rates of obesity, hypertension, type II diabetes, and heart disease, which are all associated with an unhealthful diet."

Garces and Sutherland point out the very serious side-effects from having this kind of diet:

> "Obesity and hypertension are major causes of heart disease, diabetes, kidney disease, and certain cancers. African Americans experience disproportionately high rates of obesity and hypertension, compared to whites.
>
> High blood pressure and obesity have known links to poor diet and a lack of physical activity. In the United States, the prevalence of

[5]Cristina F., and Lisa A. Sutherland. "African-American Diet." Diet.com. N.p., N.d. Web.

> high blood pressure in African Americans is among the highest in the world. The alarming rates of increase of obesity and high blood pressure, along with the deaths from diabetes-related complications, heart disease, and kidney failure, have spurred government agencies to take a harder look at these problems. As a result, many U.S. agencies have created national initiatives to improve the diet quality and the overall health of African Americans."

Over the last several years, a new term has started to surface regarding the limited healthy eating options that one can find in low-income areas. The USDA states that, "Food deserts are defined as parts of the country vapid of fresh fruit, vegetables, and other healthful whole foods, usually found in impoverished areas[6]. This is largely due to a lack of grocery stores, farmers' markets, and healthy food providers.... To qualify as a 'low-access community,' at least 500 people and/or at least 33 percent of the census tract's population must reside more than one mile from a supermarket or large grocery store (for rural census tracts, the distance is more than 10 miles)."

Michelle Obama brought the idea of a "food desert" to the forefront with her national health campaign, *Let's Move!*. She stated that, "Our goal is ambitious. It's to eliminate food deserts in America completely in seven years[7]. Sarah Corapi writes in a PBS article entitled *Why it takes more than a grocery store to eliminate a 'food desert' that the initiatives are in place*[8]:

> "Pennsylvania has launched a program whereby 88 new or expanded food retail outlets have been created, giving healthy food access to around 500,000 children and adults. And in fact, when the House passed the long-awaited farm bill on Wednesday, it included a provision for the Healthy Food Financing Initiative, which would allocate $125 million for expanding food resources in underserved communities across the nation."

[6] "Agricultural Marketing Service - Creating Access to Healthy, Affordable Food." Agricultural Marketing Service - Creating Access to Healthy, Affordable Food. USDA, N.d. Web.

[7] "Let's Move." Healthy Communities. N.p., N.d. Web. <http://www.letsmove.gov/healthy-communities>.

[8] Corapi, Sarah. "Why It Takes More than a Grocery Store to Eliminate a 'food Desert'." PBS. PBS, 3 Feb. 2014. Web.

Conversely, Corapi suggests that the success of the First Lady's plan may be more complicated than just adding more grocery stores to low-income areas. The second part of the article moves into an interview with Steven Cummins, a professor of population health at the London School of Hygiene and Tropical Medicine. He concluded that adding a store will not always compete with the comfort level that people have with their old ways of life. He gave an example of a woman that lived next to a newly established grocery store. She would still travel three miles to get her groceries at a store that she was more familiar with and had frequented throughout her life. Cummins also mentions that added choices can somewhat delude the healthy options. With so much to choose from, it can be difficult to sort through everything needed to create a healthy meal.

Overall, he had mixed feelings about the results of this study. He proposed that it could take some time for people to adapt to a new supermarket in their community. Still, he mentioned that perceptions had to change about what a normal diet should resemble. Improving access to healthy foods would not fix the problem by itself. Cummins determined that making healthy foods available is the first step, but education is the key to bridging the gap to an overall healthy lifestyle.

To muddy the waters further, Heather Tirado Gilligan wrote an article for Slate.com entitled *Food Deserts Aren't the Problem*[9]. She builds on a number of Cummins' ideas by referencing several studies on the subject:

> "A 2011 study published in the Archives of Internal Medicine showed no connection between access to grocery stores and more healthful diets using 15 years' worth of data from more than 5,000 people in five cities. One 2012 study showed that the local food environment did not influence the diet of middle-school children in California. Another 2012 study, published in Social Science and Medicine, used national data on store availability and a multiyear study of grade-schoolers to show no connection between food environment and diet. And this month, a study in Health Affairs examined one of the Philadelphia grocery stores that opened with help from the Fresh Food Financing Initiative. The authors found that the store had no significant impact

[9] Gilligan, Heather Tirado. "Getting Fresh Fruits and Vegetables Into Poor Neighborhoods Doesn't Make Poor People Healthier." Slate Magazine. N.p., 10 Feb. 2014. Web.

> on reducing obesity or increasing daily fruit and vegetable consumption in the four years since it opened."

Gilligan's article then takes a different direction from the anticipated "lack of education/supply and demand" argument.This author uniquely states that there are actually more grocery stores in poorer communities. Her culprit for the diminished health of lower-income communities is more stress related. She puts more stock in Bruce McEwen's idea of "allostatic load." This is the idea that health inequality comes from "cumulative wear and tear of stress reactions over time." Trying to come up with money for rent, school clothing, food, and heat causes more stress than the fiscal decisions made by higher-income individuals.

While there is certainly science behind the negative medical effects from stress, the dietary issues are easier to address. When comparing a change in eating habits to eliminating poverty, the latter option creates a much bigger challenge. Despite the lower concentration of grocery stores in impoverished areas, transitioning to a healthier diet does not have to be costly.

The USDA has some ideas posted on their website about eating fruits and vegetables on a budget[10]. They mention buying these items in season. This is a great way to get fruits and vegetables at the height of freshness and at the lowest price. They also suggest buying more frequently and in smaller amounts. This method prevents you from having to throw food (and money) away. Buying produce in its most simplistic form will also help people to save money. When fruits and vegetables are pre-cut or canned, it drives up the price.

There are also some more labor-intensive methods to cut costs for a healthy diet. Plant a garden. Growing fruits and vegetables takes time, but is certainly cost effective. To that end, learning to can and freeze produce will make it last longer. If there are deals to be had at the grocery store, then buy in bulk and preserve what is purchased. This strategy can also be applied to a harvested garden.

Proteins can be a little trickier, but meats are not completely off of the menu when attempting to create a healthy diet on a budget.A great article on this subject can be found on NerdFitness.com and

---

[10] "Healthy Eating on A Budget." Healthy Eating on A Budget. N.p., N.d. Web. <http://choosemyplate.gov/budget/index.html>.

is titled *Help! I'm Poor But Want to Eat Healthy*[11]!. The most consistent route to get inexpensive protein into a diet is through tuna, eggs, and beans. However, the article also points out that many meats can be bought on sale. Typically, chicken and turkey offer the most bang for your buck. Other affordable options for protein include quinoa, Greek yogurt, cottage cheese, and nut butter.

If comparing these various options with the more frequented dining alternatives in low-income areas, most would be surprised by the symmetry in cost. In fact, if a family is willing to can, freeze, and grow their own produce, the cost savings can be quite substantial. Eating healthy takes discipline and know-how. The idea of a food desert certainly carries some truth, but it is not an impossible hurdle for someone determined to eat healthy without spending and exorbitant amount of money.

Like I mentioned at the beginning of this chapter, I love Southern cooking and soul food. It is amazing and so delicious. It will always be a part of my life and diet. However, I know that it has to come in moderation and intermittently consumed within a healthier overall diet. It will literally kill someone if consumed every day at every meal.

For me, this realization came after college. I had a terrible diet through most of my teenage years and through college. However, a high metabolism and extremely athletic lifestyle kept my weight in check. As I aged, the metabolism went down and I was less active. I started to put on weight, a steady two to three pounds every year. My diet was the problem and making a change was not easy. Nevertheless, it was necessary and has made a huge impact in my life.

My changes were simple.I quit eating late at night. I put a strict 9:00 curfew on dinner. After that time, it was too late for a meal that day. I also started eating breakfast. This gave me more energy in the morning and helped me to keep my appetite in check when lunchtime came. One other giant adjustment I made was to completely eliminate my sweet tea consumption. This is no easy feat in the South. However, it was killing my diet to consume so much sugar. I basically know what I should and should not eat and try to consume more of the former while not completely shunning the latter.

[11]Taylor. "Help! I'm Poor But Want to Eat Healthy!" Nerd Fitness. N.p., 27 Dec. 2012. Web.

The soul food culture needs an update as well. It is certainly possible to have a successful life with a poor diet. I see it all the time in the banking world. However, every small improvement someone makes can help. With so many medical problems (including depression) being linked to a poor diet, the change in daily consumption can only improve someone's life.

Still, the cultural ties can be hard to break.It is tough to go against everything you have ever learned about eating. "My mom cooked this type of food. My grandmother cooked this type of food. Our ancestors cooked this type of food." There is tradition and pride in cooking recipes that are passed down for generations. This is the issue. You can surround people with healthy options, but they are going to generally default to what they know and what they are comfortable eating. White people are certainly guilty of this too. I can personally vouch for that. My wife has told me numerous times that she has walked into homes (she provided physical therapy services to low-income individuals) in impoverished areas and found the oilcan-sized Morton's salt container sitting on the owner's coffee table. Over-salting food is a problem for every demographic.

Chef Richards talked about soul food getting a more negative connotation with some African-Americans. It is thought of as fatty, unhealthy food and the only cuisine consumed in the black diet. I really enjoyed an article I read by Erika Nicole Kendell from her blog BlackGirlsGuideToWeightLoss.com[12]. It is titled Neither *Soul Food, Nor "Slave Food," Made You Fat* and makes a great argument against the idea that African-Americans are predisposed to a culture of poor eating habits.

The dietary problem developed from taking the original soul food, which was healthy and mostly vegetables, and adding unhealthy elements. Kendell talks about pan-fried chicken now being battered and deep-fried. Corn bread was not "sweet" in the origins of black cooking and it was actually used to absorb the nutrients in the water left behind after boiling vegetables. Pork was only eaten in moderation because there was not much of it and it was rationed. Soul food has evolved into the unhealthy version that is consumed today and it is mixed in with convenient fast-food and frozen dinners.

I read many articles about efforts being made to increase healthy

[12]Kendell, Erika Nicole. "Neither Soul Food, Nor "Slave Food," Made You Fat - A Black Girl's Guide To Weight Loss." A Black Girl's Guide To Weight Loss. N.p., 8 May 2013. Web.

eating knowledge in low-income communities. It is great to see that becoming so commonplace. As people begin to eat better, the demand will naturally attract grocers to their communities that provide better foods. This effort needs to continue because the culture of obesity is monumental in our country and especially in low-income areas. Eating better provides many benefits and is one cultural issue that can be corrected in a modest timeframe.

Chapter 11

The Culture of Politics

Each presidential election carries a massive understudy and examination of trends and voting demographics. Candidates position themselves to campaign in areas where they have a chance to pull electoral votes while shunning areas where they have no chance to sway public opinion. Studying voting patterns gives us a glimpse into the mind of the different demographics of this country. It is fascinating to learn how different cultures think and just how consistent they are with their political views.

CNN poling during the 2012 election gives clear insight into how the issues relate to both major parties[1]. More men voted for the Republican candidate, Mitt Romney, while more women voted for the Democratic candidate, Barack Obama. As voters age and move to higher tax brackets, they were more likely to vote Republican. Education was fairly well divided where more college graduates voted for Romney while more post-graduates voted for Obama. Candidates that were focused on the economy and budget mostly voted Republican while those focused on healthcare and foreign policy went Democrat. Of course, professed liberals and Democrats voted for Obama, while conservatives and Republicans chose Romney.

These are the most topical studies. They are understood by campaign strategists and form the skeletal design for how a candidate will tackle the huge task of running for President of the United States. There are red states and blue states and some of them rarely vote for a candidate on the other side of the aisle. For that reason, most time is spent in the confessed "swing states" where the electoral votes are up for grabs. As a professed Libertarian in the solid red state of Tennessee, I do not get to participate in or personally view much campaigning. Nonetheless, it is fun to watch on television.

It is never fair to assume that an individual votes a certain way based on the demographic that they represent. However, there are consistent trends within every demographic and this methodology works well as you move toward the law of large numbers. There

[1] "Polling Center- 2012 Election Center - Elections & Politics from CNN.com." CNN. Cable News Network, N.d. Web.

are more white people that vote Republican than vote Democrat. It is not an overwhelming margin, but there is statistical significance there. However, minorities overwhelmingly vote Democrat. In the African-American community this is above 90%.Let us take a look at the history of black voting. Unfortunately, their history is not very long.1965 by the Voting Rights Act African-Americans were not given the right to vote until 1965 by the Voting Rights Act. David Barton wrote a great timeline titled *The History of Black Voting Rights* that can be found on FreeRepublic.com [2]. He points out that the Democratic Party was not always the voice of the African-American people. During the 1856 Dred Scott decision, a Democrat-controlled Supreme Court said that blacks "had no rights which a white man was bound to respect; and that the Negro might justly and lawfully be reduced to slavery for his benefit."

In the 1700s, the laws of our nation were more state-driven. The federal government had limited power and the states were freer to make their own decisions. While blacks were not allowed to vote in national elections, some states allowed them to vote in elections at the state level. Delaware, New Hampshire, New York, Maryland, Massachusetts, and Pennsylvania granted suffrage to free-blacks to vote in state elections before the year 1800. Still, slaves were prohibited from voting in every state at this time.

Barton continues by explaining the early development of the Democratic and Republican parties. In the early 1800s, the Democratic Party was the dominant party in this country. Much of the party's popularity was due to its pro-slavery stance. In 1854, Congress became more divided on the issue and a branch broke off to form an anti-slavery party, the Republican Party.It is amazing what 150 years will do to the perception of these two groups.

This was a time of massive change in the United States. Abraham Lincoln was the first elected Republican President and slavery would be abolished. After this development, the majority of Democrats broke off from the rest of the Union and formed the Confederate States of America. This group was later granted amnesty when the war was won by the Union and would soon after participate in Congress once more.

The end of the war would not end the battle that African-Americans would have for equal rights. The feud would also continue between

[2]Barton, David. "The History of Black Voting Rights." The History of Black Voting Rights. N.p., 5 Feb. 2004. Web.

the parties over the issue of slavery. Democrats continued to work to circumvent the new laws or dismiss them altogether. Interestingly enough, Barton mentions that an African-American Representative from Mississippi said, "The opposition to civil rights in the South is confined almost exclusively to States under Democratic control. . . ." Poll taxes, literacy tests, white-only primaries, and physical intimidation were all used to limit the impact of black voting.

As we moved into the 1940s, 50s, and 60s, Democrats started to change their stance on granting voting rights to black people. The author suggests that Harry Truman was one of the very first to champion this movement. It was a struggle though. Many of his proposed changes were shot down by his own party. As the Democratic Party changed its stance on slavery, the new Southern Dixiecrat Party was born. They would continue the fight against equal rights for African-Americans.

Democrats started to make considerable waves for civil rights in 1963 under the direction of John F. Kennedy. My all-time favorite Democratic President was shot and killed before he could carry out many of his civil rights promises. Support in the party was mixed and most of his bills on the subject were either gutted or killed by a Democrat-led Congress. Lyndon Johnson continued Kennedy's efforts, but with only modest support from his own party, he needed Republican backing as well. The parties worked together (for maybe the last time) to produce the 1964 Civil Rights Bill, followed by the 1965 Voting Rights Act.

David Barton still suggests that the Republican Party should be the party of the African-American people. He does not feel that circumstances have changed to warrant the overt support that Democrats receive from the black community. Barton mentions the famous Frederick Douglas quote, "The Republican Party is the ship, all else is the sea." While the author makes some excellent arguments, it is clear that the Republican Party is no longer even close to being the African-American party of choice.

The black support for Republicans took its first blow under Franklin Roosevelt. The website, MillerCenter.org illustrates the situation for black American in the 1930s[3]:

---

[3] "Miller Center." American President: Franklin Delano Roosevelt: The American Franchise. N.p., N.d. Web.

> "One important demographic change underlay the experience of African-Americans during the Roosevelt years. The migration of African- Americans from the South to the urban North, which began in 1910, continued in the 1930s and accelerated in the 1940s during World War II. As a result, black Americans during the Roosevelt years lived for the most part either in the urban North or in the rural South, although the Depression chased increasingly large numbers of blacks to southern cities as well. In the North, blacks encountered de facto segregation, racism, and discrimination in housing and public services; nevertheless, they were able to vote and had better job opportunities. In the South, blacks were disfranchised, lived under a segregationist regime enforced by violence, and found fewer avenues for escape from crushing poverty."

Although, African-Americans did not always receive the social services promised by the New Deal, they were occasionally getting something to help with the aftermath of the Great Depression. This was a stark contrast to having no safety net at all. The website also maintains that FDR was against many of the laws that were blatantly standing against equal rights. However, he did not voice many of them because that would have cost him the much needed white vote in the South. Jesse Merkel of PolicyMic.com wrote that, "In 1936, Roosevelt was able to get 71% of the black vote, a devastating blow to Republicans. The GOP was able to make some gains back during the 1950s under President Eisenhower, but the next decade would see the final nail in the coffin."

So, what caused this seemingly permanent change? Obviously, Kennedy's efforts were appreciated. He had made the biggest push for equal rights since Lincoln. Bill O'Reilly wrote a great book called *Kennedy's Last Days* that is full of pictures and stories about the President working closely with Martin Luther King, Jr. [4] Working hand-in-hand with the greatest of civil rights leaders was a powerful statement and Democrats became the party of equality. It did not matter that the Republicans were instrumental in actually getting the legislation passed. Like the French in the American Revolution, they may have had a dramatic impact in the ultimate conclusion, but the Colonists still get credit for the victory.

[4] O'Reilly, Bill. "Kennedy's Last Days: The Assassination That Defined a Generation." Henry Holt and Co. (BYR), 11 June 2013. Web.

Tiffany Gabbay has an article on Blaze.com entitled *Why Did the Black Community Leave the GOP for the Democratic Party?*[5] She mentions another factor that is a black-eye for Republicans. Nixon ran with a "Southern Strategy" in 1948. The feeling was that Nixon was going to help support segregation in the South by allowing them to secure stronger state's rights. This would secure the white, Southern vote for his presidency. After Kennedy, Johnson, and Nixon, African-Americans were firm supporters of the Democratic Party.

While difficult for anyone to cast a vote for a candidate that completely encompasses his or her exact feelings on every political issue, it is interesting to compare and contrast cultural leanings with party stances. I have a friend that made his father take a test on that very subject not long ago. His father answered the questions and then was given a conclusion derived from his answers. It told him which party he should vote for and why. Oddly, he had been voting for a party that disagreed with many of his most important personal philosophies.

My point for this story is not to necessarily agree with Mr. Barton that African-Americans should vote Republican, but there are some key contradictions in their allegiance to the Democratic Party. One such issue is gay-marriage. Democrats have been historically supportive of gay-marriage, but African-Americans adamantly disagree on the subject (at an almost 90% clip). One of the more interesting juxtapositions in our country is the struggle that a classically liberal state like California has had in passing same-sex marriage laws. The melting pot of that state has two major headwinds, Hispanics and African-Americans.

Both are deeply religious and socially conservative. For that reason, both demographics are mostly against gay marriage and abortion. Dan Merica of CNN wrote an article entitled *Survey: Among black, Hispanic Americans, complexity reigns on abortion issue*, which looked at this commonality [6]. He mentioned that attitudes are relaxing a bit with each new generation. However, Merica states that, "A strong majority of Hispanic - 84% - and black Americans - 68% - who hear about the abortion issue in church responded that their clergy say abortion is 'morally wrong'."

---

[5] Gabbay, Tiffany. "Why Did the Black Community Leave the GOP for the Democratic Party?" The Blaze. N.p., 7 Sept. 2012. Web.

[6] Merica, Dan. "Survey: Among Black, Hispanic Americans, Complexity Reigns on Abortion Issue." CNN Belief Blog RSS. N.p., 26 July 2012. Web.

With the social agenda being fairly similar to the Republican Party, the dedication that both races have to the Democratic Party must be fiscally oriented, right? Somewhat. I read numerous surveys on the subject that mentioned how neither demographic feels like the Republican Party cares about them. Nine out of ten Republican voters are white and that is a trend that is likely to continue.

Democrats solidify their party's allegiance of Hispanics and African-Americans because of a few very specific issues. For Hispanics, the key issue is immigration. The Democratic Party has done a great job of labeling themselves as the more inclusive party. With the Republican Party showing more focus on closing the border and eliminating social services for illegal immigrants, they have cost themselves many Hispanic voters through the years. As I discussed earlier, the issue for African-Americans is equality. Once again, this demographic has been won over by the idea of inclusion. Furthermore, with the poverty suffered within both races in this country, the Democratic Party generally promises more social services like healthcare, food stamps, and welfare.

More affluent Hispanics and African-Americans are more likely to vote Republican when compared to the less affluent members of their race. Nevertheless, they are still more likely to vote Democrat than not. Even though they are likely to side with the social and religious issues supported by Republicans, the key swing issues are immigration, equality, and social services. The abortion and gay-marriage issues are not important enough to change their minds. They both generally feel that Democrats are there to help the poor, while Republicans are self-serving and neglect those in need. According to Brooks Jackson's article, *Blacks and the Democratic Party* on FactCheck.org,[7] "....Johnson signed the 1965 Voting Rights Act. No Republican presidential candidate has gotten more than 15 percent of the black vote since."In 2008, *The Washington Post* did a poll called *Voters on why blacks pick* Democrats [8]. They compared different reasons among Republican, Democrats, and Independents (the numbers are raw counts and not percentages—over 1,000 people were surveyed).

[7] Jackson, Brooks. "Blacks and the Democratic Party." FactCheck.org. N.p., 18 Apr. 2008. Web.

[8] "Voters on Why Blacks Pick Democrats." The Washington Post, 29 Aug. 2012. Web.

Democrats	answered:
48	Issues of poverty/help poor/represent the little guy
35	More helpful to African Americans
35	Party represents average people/workers over businesses
29	Issues of civil rights/helps minorities
16	Democrats more helpful to society as a whole
Republican	answered:
59	Government dependents/want something for nothing/welfare
36	Supportive of welfare/entitlements
17	Parents voted Democratic/taught to vote Democratic
16	Uninformed/ignorant/uneducated
15	More helpful to African Americans
Independents	answered:
31	Supportive of entitlements/welfare/healthcare
26	Government dependents/want something for nothing/welfare
24	Issues of poverty/help poor/represent the little guy
23	More helpful to African Americans
20	Issue of civil rights/help minorities

Will the trend of black voters siding with Democratic candidates continue into the future? It is highly probable, but there are some interesting developments to consider.Ben Adler wrote an article on Progressive.org entitled *40 More Years: How the Democrats Will Rule the Next Generation*[9]. In the article, he notes the outpour of support that Barack Obama had from the black community:

[9] Adler, Ben. "40 More Years: How the Democrats Will Rule the Next Generation | The Progressive." The Progressive. N.p., 09 June 2009. Web.

> "(James) Carville triumphantly notes that blacks made up 13 percent of the electorate in 2008, versus 11 percent in 2004, and that 96 percent of blacks voted for Obama, without even acknowledging that voting for the first black President is an unusual circumstance. If Democrats simply assume that their level of support and turnout from African Americans will be that high for the next forty years, they may be in for a disappointment. After all, the percentage of blacks voting Democratic was lower for Al Gore and John Kerry."

The author indicates that the surge in support may have been more for the man than for the party in the 2008 election. Barack Obama was wildly popular within the African-American community and with younger people. Adler is not ready to claim that the younger generation is leaning as heavily to the Democratic Party as their voting in that election might indicate. Also, it was a very exciting time for black Americans to have the opportunity to vote for the very first black President. I can remember Jermaine telling me how his entire family was jumping around while watching the election coverage. They could not believe that a black man was taking over the highest office in the land.

Peter Levine wrote a curious article for TheRoot.com entitled *Young, Black and Voting*. In the article, he talks about young voter turnout [10]. Mr. Levine points out that, "In 2008 young African Americans set an all-time voter-turnout record. Fifty-eight percent of black 18- to 29-year-olds voted – the highest rate that any ethnic or racial group of young adults has ever achieved." He noted that generally voter turn-out is a reflection of affluence. Being comparable with young white voters in this area is an indication that black voters are more politically engaged (the assumption being that the average, young white voter is also wealthier and is more predisposed to voting).

As I read his article, I noticed that there were several examinations into why the other young, black voters did not make it to the booths in 2008. The overwhelming answer was that the Democratic Party did not do enough nationally or at the state level to promote African-American voter turnout. Levine did not mention Republicans at all. The indication is that if a black person votes, he or she will vote Democrat. It almost goes without stating.

I expect this trend to continue for the foreseeable future for a number of reasons. While African-Americans represent a formidable de-

[10] Levine, Peter. "Black Youth Voter Turnout: 2012 Not Guaranteed." The Root. N.p., 2 Dec. 2011. Web.

mographic that could help either party, they will not be included in the Republican strategy anytime soon. Romney was caught admitting this reality during a campaign speech. The platform of low taxes, pro-life, pro-God, and lower spending just does not resonate like the Democratic pitch. This is a battle that the Republicans see as unwinnable and they may choose to focus their resources elsewhere.

Where, you might ask? The Hispanic vote will probably get the majority of the Republican focus. We have already seen a few trends that allude to that strategy. The GOP has lightened its stance on immigration and amnesty. They already corner the market for pro-life and pro-God stances and they are also putting more emphasis on viable Hispanic candidates—notably Marco Rubio. While whites are still the majority today, census projections see that coming to an end by 2043. At that point, the black and Hispanic populations are collectively projected to surpass the white majority. Hispanics will more than likely double the African-American vote though.

It is difficult to look too far out into the future for trends and voting. Not only do parties change (as we have examined in this chapter), but people and demographics change. It will not be as easy in the future to go after the "black vote" or "white vote." We are becoming more and more diverse as a people because of interracial dating/marriage as well as more complex thinking. Everyone seems to have their own unique political stance and many of them post about it openly on Facebook (which facilitates an exchange of ideas that we have never experienced before)

Unfortunately, in the meantime, this means that white and Hispanic voters will get the most emphasis from our two major parties. African-Americans will be accepted by both parties, but will not necessarily be a priority. As a steady draw to the Democratic side, African-American allegiance will make "black-focused" legislation less frequent because they will not be the squeaky wheel needing the grease. If an issue is near to the heart of the African-American community, it will likely take a back seat to white and Hispanic concerns.

For this reason, it will be increasingly important for African- Americans to blaze their own paths. While I would extend this same advice to anyone, regardless of race, African-Americans will not be able to rely on the government to organize their people or eliminate their problems. As politicians focus more and more on trends, the black community will continue to be the “odd man out”. It will be fascinating to monitor how long their affinity for the Democratic Party lasts. Change seems to be the only political constant and I certainly expect the cultural draw to evolve as younger generations become more involved in the voting process.

Chapter 12

Dress and Success

While language is probably the biggest hurdle when immersing oneself into another culture, clothing is the most immediately noticeable aspect of being in a foreign land. If you were ever dropped randomly into another country, looking to see what everyone is wearing would be the first step to figuring out where you are. In some countries, it might be tough to tell because they are on the cutting edge and always working to keep track of the latest trends and styles. However, other countries may dress in accordance to religion, climate, or a strict adherence to tradition.

Susanne Kuchler and Daniel Miller wrote a book on the topic titled *Clothing as Material Culture*[1]. They argue that:

> "Cloth and clothing are living, vibrant parts of culture and the body. From the recycling of cloth in Africa and India and the use of pattern in the Pacific, to the history of 'wash and wear' and why women wear the wrong clothes to restaurants in London, this book shows the considerable advantage gained by seamlessly combining material and social aspects of dress and textiles."

Their book takes a look at the relationship between the textiles that are available as well as the purpose for the clothing of the area.

China has a fascinating diversity of clothing within its culture. I have really enjoyed reading Martin Jacques book, *When China Rules the World*[2]. Jacques covers the many different styles used throughout that land. Some dress to work. They could be farmers, factory workers, or businessmen. China is also one of the oldest countries in the world and they have a keen understanding of their history and try to incorporate their traditions into their progress. Traditional dress is still common, especially in ceremonies like parades and marriage. China's myriad of different styles of dress sets them

[1] Kuchler, Susanne, and Daniel Miller. "Clothing as Material Culture." Bloomsbury Academic, 12 May 2005. Web.

[2] Jacques, Martin. "When China Rules the World: The End of the Western World and the Birth of a New Global Order." Penguin Books, 28 Aug. 2012. Web.

apart and creates a unique clothing culture that is only rivaled by a few other countries.

Clothing is also used to indicate one's status within the community. In many countries, certain colors are reserved for royalty. There may also be particular objects that may only be worn by people of a definite class, like a crown for example. Even if a country does not formally mandate a dress-code among the classes, this differentiation can still happen. More impoverished citizens will naturally buy or make less expensive clothes from the materials that are available. Wealthier citizens will have more exotic or imported materials because of their financial clout and access.

We will take a closer look at social mobility in chapter 13, but clothing is a complimentary aspect of moving up the socioeconomic ladder. The old saying goes, "Dress for the job you want and not for the job that you have." Scott Reeves wrote an article for *Forbes Magazine* entitled *Dress for Success* [3]. He talks about some of the basic items that a man should wear to impress those around him in a job setting. Reeves says that a "button down shirt," "polished black shoes," "a blue, black or grey jacket," and "slacks that complement the jacket" are all traditional working attire. Dressing professionally and conservatively is the key to a successful interview and career.

I feel comfortable in assuming that Jermaine does not have any of these essential items in his closet. Once, I cleaned out my closet, looking for items that did not fit or that I just no longer wore regularly. Instead of taking them to Goodwill, I gave them to Jermaine. The only item that I ever saw him wear from a pile of clothes is a Nike polo-style shirt. If something is not his style, it is completely okay by me for him to not wear it. Still, I wanted him to have some nicer clothes in his closet should he ever need to dress more formally. I am not sure that anything ever made it there. I never asked him what he did with the clothes. They were a gift and his to do with what he liked.

While many middleclass and wealthy people would agree that having a quality suit or a few nice pieces of clothing are a good investment for a poor person, they are typically perplexed by some other purchases. Tressie McMillan Cottom wrote an article for TalkingPointsMemo.com titled *Why Do Poor People 'Waste' Money On Lux-*

[3] Reeves, Scott. "Dress For Success." Forbes Magazine, 12 Apr. 2006. Web.

ury Goods? [4]. In it, she illustrates the point of a clothing investment in more unconventional ways. Cottom tells a story about her mother accompanying a friend to the welfare office to get aid because the lady was suddenly raising a granddaughter. The woman had battled with the office for over a year without making any headway. Cottom's mother dressed well and presented herself professionally to the decision makers of the office in an attempt to help her friend. By doing this, she got results for her in a matter of hours.

Cottom continues by mentioning other "dividends" resulting from her mother's investment in clothing and jewelry. In addition to standing apart in the social service office, she noticed different treatment from her school's principal. Her mother was not to be taken for granted. She may not have been able to afford many nice things, but worked a few nice items into her budget for important occasions.

The author then moves into the psychological motives for living above one's means. "We want to belong," she writes. Dressing nicely can make a person feel good, but it can also be the difference in getting or not getting a job. Presentation does matter and a person needs to dress the part if they expect to be rewarded. Cottom understood this and she explained that her neat presentation served her well in job interviews.

> "There is empirical evidence that women and people of color are judged by appearances differently and more harshly than are white men. What is remarkable is that these gatekeepers told me the story. They wanted me to know how I had properly signaled that I was not a typical black or a typical woman, two identities that in combination are almost always conflated with being poor."

The author makes an interesting observation that luxury items are the keys to get by the gatekeepers. These are the people standing in the way of a person getting a job, loan, or admittance to a "club" that is currently off-limits to him or her. If people want others to assume they are successful, they must dress like they are successful. It can be difficult to get the high paying job and then alter one's lifestyle accordingly. In this situation, the cart must come before the horse.

[4] Cottom, Tressie McMillan. "Why Do Poor People 'Waste' Money On Luxury Goods?" Talking Points Memo. N.p., 1 Nov. 2013. Web.

When I was in college, one of my white friends motioned toward a well-dressed black student. He asked if I had ever noticed how *they* were always "dressed to the nines." Honestly, I had never thought about it until then. All of the African-Americans that I grew up with dressed like I did for the most part. I had not reached the point in my life where anyone made enough money to make a conscious decision about their wardrobe. I was around plenty of rich, white kids and poor, white kids. I could notice the difference between poor and rich, but nothing more.

As I worked my way through college and then entered the workforce after graduation, I started to notice this phenomenon more and more. My black colleagues dress very well—certainly better than I do. I remember working with a black gentleman that wore a suit every day to the bank. We were not required to wear a suit and would typically dress down a bit on Fridays. It did not matter to him. He always wore a suit to work. I also had an African-American client that I always respected for his formality in the bank. He wore a derby-style hat and would remove it before entering. He had to use a walker to move around, but was too much of a gentleman to not stop, brace himself, and remove his hat before entering the building.

Michel Martin of WWNO.org conducted an interview on this very subject [5]. The transcript on their website is titled *Why Black Men Tend To Be Fashion Kings.* Martin makes the observation that, "For many, style is much deeper than articles of clothing; it's a statement of identity. Black men have a unique relationship with fashion, one that can be traced all the way back to the 17th and 18th centuries." The interview is conducted with Monica Miller and Victor Holliday. Miller is an associate professor of English at Barnard College and Holliday is an associate producer of on-air fundraising at NPR.

Miller explains, "African-American men have used style as a way to challenge stereotypes about who they are. 'Sometimes the well-dressed black man coming down the street is asking you to look and think'." Holliday had the comment, "Because as you present yourself seriously, people tend to take you seriously." He mentions that he got this outlook from his father and can even remember his first trench coat and top hat. This dapper tradition being passed from father to son does not surprise me. I have worked with many black

[5] Martin, Michel. "Why Black Men Tend To Be Fashion Kings." WWNO. N.p., 2 Jan. 2013. Web.

gentlemen that still wear a formal hat. Occasionally, I will see an older white man wearing a hat, but not often.

Holiday mentions that dressing properly is a strategy and he relates it back to Martin Luther King, Jr. He "had a suit and a tie and a crisp, white shirt on as he was leading the struggle for civil rights and you see people of color just dressed so well, you wanted to bring your best self forward and be in appearance like you were taking care of business because they certainly were." When asked if black men ever take their style too far (overdress), Holiday said:

> "I can't say that anybody's actually said that in that sort of direct way. Maybe perhaps somebody has thought that, but I know that, when I step out of my door, I want to put my best foot forward. Obviously, we've had a certain kind of history in this country. And like my parents and their parents before them, which had very little to work with - I mean, they had a few glad rags to wear, but they took care of those things and they were an important way to earn a better way in the world because you had to be concerned about somebody's perception.
>
> We just enjoy our clothes and I think, for some of us, it's just a way of, I think, being more present, respected, perceived in a certain light in the greater society and it was a quicker way to really, sort of, step up."

Monica Miller wrote a book entitled *Slaves to Fashion: Black Dandyism and the Styling of Black Diasporic Identity*[6]. Miller elaborates on the idea of standing apart through the clothing that one wears:

> That initial moment of black dandyism also includes not only just that kind of moment in which black people were dressed to be objects, but at the same kind of exact time, black men in particular - they learned how to appropriate or, kind of, to, kind of, flip the script - if we want to talk about it in a black tradition - flipped the script on that particular mode of degradation. So, as soon as white masters put their black slaves into this fancy dress, the black slaves realized - huh, clothing means something. I might be able to put - you know, to really restyle it in a way that might allow me to say something slightly different about myself that perhaps my master is not necessarily anticipating.

[6]Miller, Monica L. "Slaves to Fashion: Black Dandyism and the Styling of Black Diasporic Identity." Duke University Press, 8 Oct. 2009. Web.

The idea is simple. People place others into a category based on appearance. If someone wants to be placed in a particular grouping, they have to look like they belong in that sort. If one wants to be treated well, they must dress well. The other option is to not be taken seriously and dismissed. This market is not cornered exclusively by African-Americans. There are many other cultures that traditionally put a lot of effort into their style and appearance and it happens all over the world. Italian, French, Japanese, and many other countries are extremely fashion-conscious.

When Jermaine was younger, I would generally give him money or a gift card of some sort for his birthday and Christmas. I was never really sure where the cash would go and preferred giving gift cards. His mom would usually get him an outfit and he would be really proud of it. That difference in culture fascinated me because I never liked getting clothes as a gift when I was that age. I always wanted a toy or something that I could play with outside. Of course, I would regularly receive school clothes and other necessities that were not considered gifts. The difference may not be 100% cultural. As Jermaine grew older, he told his mom to stop getting him clothes and to save her money.

Clothing and style are an important part of African-American culture. Many wear formal hats or baseball caps that have desirable colors or logos. The team represented is an afterthought many times. In a business setting, suits can be traditional or have more flair. I have seen different shades of yellow and brown that are more uncommon in typical white dress as well as five or more buttons on the suit. Black men and women also wear shoes that are unique in style and material. While much of the white community feels more comfortable blending in with the surrounding people, black people do not seem to mind standing out a bit.

There are certainly cultural differences when it comes to the way that people dress. It can be quite striking at times. Much of the black community has a great understanding of the importance of presentation. They are ahead of most other cultures in our country in this regard. Proper dressing is a consistent theme along the entire socioeconomic spectrum for African-Americans. Even the poorest black people take pride and care in their dress. This is an area where culture serves them extremely well and gives them an advantage over most other demographics.

Part III

Generational Mistakes

Chapter 13

Social Mobility and Economic Success

When examining cyclical poverty, it is important to study the typical tendencies of people that have generational success. Some like to equate financial success to a level of work ethic. The harder you work, the more you will make. This book's study takes a different approach. Certainly, harder work will generally produce better results given your personal situation. However, this notion is frequently criticized. Some individuals work incredibly hard throughout their lives, but never reach the wealth that other people may have that generally work a more leisurely schedule.

Why should someone that works a grinding existence see less financial success than someone that has a less-intense experience? The convenient answer is to say that others have it easy. They either inherited the money or they simply belong to the right demographic. In this case, white-male would be the most advantageous while black-female would be the most difficult. As you look at the numbers in regard to frequency of success, it is hard to challenge this idea. This chapter will delve into this issue and peel back the layers of the onion further.I will not deny that some demographics have a more challenging climb on the socioeconomic ladder. The important contradiction is that I believe it is possible to make the ascent despite all disadvantages that one might inherit at birth.

Making financial progress may take a completely different mindset than that of your parents. Hard work is a significant part of the equation and cannot be taken for granted. Still, there are also many other life choices that need to be made in order for *hard work* to gain traction. Without these items in place, it becomes increasingly difficult to blaze your path toward financial success. A person will not only have to develop a strong work ethic, but they may also need to form their own opinions about resisting urges and conforming to their community's standards.When closely examined, changing a person's thought process appears to be the more difficult hurdle. This is exemplified by my experience with BBBS.

Jermaine was and is a promising young man. I have always liked him and know that he has the potential to rise above his situation. What I did not know, until recently, is that overcoming the influence of his community would be his toughest challenge. I naively thought that by seeing the relative success that I had at an early age, he would want to emulate my life. It has been quite the awakening for me to find out that he would slide into the exact same circumstances as those around him.

The first glaring issue facing the more impoverished communities of this country is the challenge of raising a child as a single parent. Raising a child with a significant other is difficult, but going it alone is one of the most financially crippling situations one can find himself (or, more typically, herself) trying to navigate. According to the 2006 Census, there are over 13 million single parents in the United States [1]. The Department of Agriculture estimated in 2010 that it costs on average almost $227,000 to raise a child [2]. The average income of a high school graduate, is a little more than $20,000 annually. The simple math in this equation presents the unmanageable task at hand.

As you may have perceived, many single parents do live below the poverty line. The financial responsibilities are virtually impossible to traverse, but there are many psychological issues that accompany this predicament as well. Those living below the poverty line are more inclined to develop depression, anxiety, and other health issues. This can lead to numerous problems, the most damaging being a poor relationship with his or her child.As you can see, this is how the cycle begins and continues. Parents in this situation are against the odds and they have the most difficult time properly raising a child.

I want to make sure that readers understand that this book is not being judgmental of any situation. On the contrary, the idea is to point out perceived behaviors that lead to financial distress and attempt to break that generational cycle. According to a 2013 report by the Pew Research Center, over 60% of single parents made less than $30,000 annually [3]. This is a systemic trial and the numbers

---

[1] "Financial Tips for Single Parents." Midland National Life Insurance Company. N.p., 11 June 2014. Web.

[2] Bjega, Alan. "Cost to Raise 2010 U.S. Newborn Is $226,920." Bloomberg, 9 June 2011. Web.

[3] Halpin, John. "Why Single Mothers Are In Economic Crisis And What Can Be

are clear. If the first step to getting help is admitting that you have a problem, then the first step to improving the life of your family is to admit that they are making consistent mistakes with each passing generation.

The concept of "social mobility" becomes a glaring obstacle. How is Na'Licia, who had a child at 17, and then two others, going toI want to make sure that move up the social ladder? It appears to be an impossible task. Harvard economist Raj Chetty said that, "children of married parents also have higher rates of upward mobility if they live in communities with fewer single parents [4]."So, not only does it help your cause to have two parents, but it is also statistically better for children to live in a community that has less single parents.

The more telling statistic may be that poorer people living in clusters are less likely to leave the cluster. In the rare instance that a single parent living below the poverty line lives within a wealthy community (some wealthy areas can have pockets of government housing for example), Dr. Chetty has found that they would be more likely to experience social mobility.

Another answer seems obvious. If wealthy surroundings and increased income create more opportunity, then the redistribution of wealth from the very wealthy to the very poor is the cure. Peculiarly, this solution does not have statistical support. His findings actually indicated that a strong two-parent home and better schools were the solution. Taxing and throwing money at the poor was somewhat inconsequential. It is becoming a more consistent occurrence that funding, devoted to solving problems, is having minimal impact. Unfortunately, the solutions are far more complicated and tedious.

There were some other finds in Dr. Chetty's study that had statistical significance. When there is a higher frequency of voting and devout religious affiliation in the area, children are more likely to experience social moves. As a *laissez faire* economist, I do not typically push religion in my writing. However, I would be remiss to not include its impact. The relationship between voluntary community involvement and the progress of that area are important. Churches do amazing work in their communities and generally have a more

Done About It." Think Progress. N.p., 18 Mar. 2013. Web.

[4] Raj, Chetty. "Upward Mobility In America." On Point with Tom Ashbrook. NPR, 23 July 2013. Web.

lasting impression than a government project. This is due to the consistency and frequency of their work and funding.

If a single parent home presents the greatest economic challenge, then what demographic creates the situation that is most likely to succeed? As you might expect, the *answer* is a couple that lives together, shares expenses, and does not have children. Coincidentally, another Harvard professor, Dr. Daniel Gilbert, studied that couples are also happier without children [5]. I mention this only because of the juxtaposition that a young, single parent might experience with depression and anxiety. "Figures show that married people are in almost every way happier than unmarried people – whether they are single, divorced, cohabiting," comments Dr. Gilbert. He went on to add that, "They are healthier, live longer, have more sex."

If a couple makes the leap to procreate, the first thought is that children are a lot of work and responsibility. So, of course that stress will naturally take its toll. Still, your parenting issues go further than that and many can be quantified. The financial issues of paying for a child are evident. Your transition is the move from having two incomes and low expenses to having to make a tough financial decision: Do you move down to one income with increased expenses or do you stick with two incomes and add yet another considerable expense–daycare? When you start looking at the expense side of the equation, the occasional missed date night, forgone weekend sleeping in, or missed weekend getaway seem trivial.

To further explore this point, it would be helpful to have a substantial test group that is full of couples without children.Luckily (for this study), there is a segment of the population like this: the gay community. This portion of the population is full of dual-income, no kid (DINK) relationships. According to a 2012 survey of over 1,000 gay couples by Prudential, there were several financial advantages found [6]. On average, gay couples made more money, had a lower unemployment rate, saved more, and struggled with less debt. This financial success occurs without the assistance of being able to legally marry in most places. To further the point, homosexuals also have a better average education.

[5] Kate, Devlin. "Marriage without Children the Key to Bliss." The Telegraph. Telegraph Media Group, 09 May 2008. Web.

[6] "LGBT Financial Experience 2012-2013 Research Study | Prudential." Prudential, N.d. Web. <http://www.prudential.com/lgbt>.

Lacking the responsibility inherent with having a child has significant long-run advantages when furthering your education or career. Women have struggled with this obstacle for centuries. Even after Kennedy's Equal Pay Act of 1963, women still make less than 80% on average of what a man would make doing the same job [7]. In this day and age, it is difficult to feel like the difference is due to blatant sexism. The discrepancy in pay comes down to a risk/reward relationship. Women are the higher risk to cut their careers short or take significant time off from work.

The reality is not fair and it is not my intent to take a political stance on the issue. My point in bringing this situation up is to illustrate that companies are taking into account the threat of children when paying their employees. Unless there is a fundamental biological change within our species, the problem of women being paid unfairly will continue to persist. Hiring a woman presents extra risks to a company and they mitigate that risk by passing some of the economic cost along to the employee.

What about the women that do not have children? Well, this situation is interesting! American Enterprise Institute scholar Christina Hoff Sommers has uncovered some surprising statistics. She found that women without children often earn more money than their male counterparts [8]. In fact, in a comparison of unmarried and childless men and women between the ages of 35 and 43, women earn more: 108 cents on a man's dollar. She also found that some of the unequal pay statistics can be misleading because many women pursue humanities based careers. Occupations in that arena generally pay less than the math and science fields that frequently draw more men.

The overwhelming message received by these findings is that opportunity comes from not having children, at least not right away. I am certainly not advocating never having children. However, it generally makes sense to delay procreation. It financially benefits couples as well as individuals to abstain for a while.As an economist, it may be easier for me to look at the numbers before making life decisions. Regardless, it does make sense to at least consider the financial impact of having children *before* reproducing. People are living

[7]Coy, Peter, and Elizabeth Dwoskin. "Shortchanged: Why Women Get Paid Less Than Men." Bloomberg Business Week. N.p., 21 June 2012. Web.

[8]Furchtgott-Roth, Diana. "Christina Hoff Sommers' 'Freedom Feminism' Is Right Path for Women's Movement." Washington Examiner. N.p., 18 June 2013. Web.

longer and staying healthier longer. It is possible to have children well into your 30s and 40s and waiting makes the financial challenge of having children more palatable.

Laura Sandler wrote a controversial article for *Time Magazine* entitled *Having It All Without Having Children*[9]. She states that the U.S. birthrate is the lowest it has ever been and this even includes the "fertility crash" of the Great Depression. In that article she also cites a study that was conducted at the London School of Economics by Satoshi Kanazawa. He found that more intelligent women (as determined by IQ) are waiting longer and longer to have children, or not having them at all. To further perpetuate the theme, women that wait longer and are further into their careers (and presumably better educated) have an even higher opportunity cost to have children. Delay seems to have a bit of a spiraling effect. The longer you wait, the more you give up to have children.

Naturally, there are some concerns about waiting. The first to come to mind is the ever-present biological clock. It is ticking and women are well aware of it. They see it on television and many are reminded of it by their families. The good news is that there are many options available to *older* women planning to have children. Fertility drugs have come a long way and allow many women to become pregnant well into their 40s. Of course, adoption is always a wonderful alternative. There are thousands of children that need parents and they are not nearly as picky about your age as one might think.

Unfortunately for Na'Licia and many other women living in poverty, she has made a critical decision that will continue to present challenges to her social mobility. She has put herself in the same position as Chastity and Charlotte when they were her age. Having children early in life and before settling with a significant other is the most difficult path to financial success. Now, her options are more limited. She has children to take care of and it will be a challenge for her to maintain consistent employment.

One basic economic principle is that people respond to incentives. Somehow, we need to find a way to remove the incentive to have children at such a young age. The current pressures are legitimate on a young woman in Na'Licia's community. If you have a child, it gives you the ability to start drawing government assistance, which can be a means to move out on your own. We also have to remember

[9] Sandler, Laura. "Having It All Without Having Children." Time. N.p., 12 Aug. 2013. Web.

that in impoverished communities, many children are exposed to mature subject matter. This accelerates the process and comfort level in a person becoming sexually active. It is incredibly difficult to steer someone away from teenage pregnancy when it is accepted by your peers, rewarded by the government, and common within your own family.

The National Center for Chronic Disease Prevention and Health Promotion found in 2008 that 435,000 live births occurred to mothers between the ages of 15 and 19 [10]. More than half of those births were unintended. They estimate that teen pregnancies cost the tax payers more than $9 billion between "increased health care and foster care, increased incarceration rates among children of teen parents, and lost tax revenue because of lower educational attainment and income among teen mothers."

The CDC lists teen pregnancy as one of its top six priorities. This is a list of the specific ways where they would like to encourage a change in the thought process of at-risk teenagers:

1. Knowledge of sexual issues, HIV, other STDs, and pregnancy (including methods of prevention).
2. Perception of HIV risk.
3. Personal values about sex and abstinence.
4. Attitudes toward condoms (pro and con).
5. Perception of peer norms and behavior about sex.
6. Individual ability to refuse sex and to use condoms.
7. Intent to abstain from sex, or limit number of partners.
8. Communication with parents or other adults about sex, condoms, and contraception.
9. Individual ability to avoid HIV/STD risk and risk behaviors.
10. Avoidance of places and situations that might lead to sex.
11. Intent to use a condom.

[10] Preventing Teen Pregnancy 2010-2015 (n.d.): n. pag. CDC.gov. Centers for Disease Control. Web. <http://www.cdc.gov/TeenPregnancy/PDF/TeenPregnancy_AAG.pdf>.

Changing attitudes, cultures, and lifestyles can be incredibly difficult. Ideally, it would be more effective to provide incentives to not become pregnant. The issue of welfare to mothers is a double-edged sword. On one side, we are providing much needed assistance to a young woman that has limited alternatives. On the other, we are enabling men and women to make irresponsible decisions. Cutting this element of welfare would undoubtedly make a significant impact in reducing teen pregnancies. However, it would also be a harsh reality for anyone that managed to find themselves in that very predicament.

The more liberal answer of handing out contraception is gaining some traction. Most conservatives, especially social conservatives, and religious voters do not like the idea of paying for contraception. The idea creates a direct conflict with their religious beliefs. It is also viewed as another tax for a program that promotes irresponsible behavior. While this logic is true, the net savings to the tax payers would be significant with government sponsored birth control. It would certainly lessen the cost and long-term concerns associated with teen pregnancy.Ironically, I could see many fiscal conservatives being onboard with this idea.

I also wonder if medical science will assist us with this issue one day. I envision a science-fiction movie where all babies receive a reversible procedure that prevents them from reproducing. It has the effect of a vasectomy or hysterectomy and is minimally invasive. When two people decide that they are ready to have children, they visit the doctor and have the switch turned on for procreation. Voila–no more unwanted pregnancies.

Outside of this crazy notion, this situation is difficult to regulate and improve. The ideal situation is for communities to start really putting thought into their reproduction and financial futures. Young people need to know how difficult life is with a child and exactly how detrimental that situation can be as a teenager. This is an extremely tough code to crack and women like Charlotte, Chastity, and Na'Licia will continue to struggle with its consequences for some time.

Chapter 14

Childhood Development

I mentioned earlier that I met Jermaine when he was 12 years old. After my interview with him, I wondered if I had met him too late to truly make an impact. Would it have made a difference if I had starting working with him while he was in kindergarten or even earlier? I certainly have some regrets, but most of them are based on his current unemployment status. I had much higher hopes for him and it saddens me deeply that he has been unable to work toward his potential (not that I am giving up just yet).

I am working my way through Pimsleur's Hungarian lessons on CD. Each lesson is about 25 minutes long and that is the perfect length for my drive home from work. I turn on the lesson and work my way through it as I head south out of the city of Nashville toward my home in Franklin, TN. My father and aunt are Hungarian and so I have had substantial exposure to the language. However, it is not an easy task to learn a new language as an adult. In fact, I have heard that it is far easier to learn as a child and feel like I needed a better understanding of that phenomenon.

One of my colleagues has a Thai wife. Their son can speak both English and Thai fluently. They have friends whose families are comprised of the same arrangement of one Thai partner and one American partner. When their children get together they interact by using both languages. They seamlessly move between Thai and English with ease, using the word or phrase from the selected language that does the best job of expressing their intentions. It is amazing!

So, what would be the ideal age to start working with an at-risk child? I started to look for answers and came across the *Child Development Tracker on PBS.org* [1]. The site is divided into different subjects and the tracker will tell you some general developments that children will experience in those areas as they age. As mentioned before, math and science are typically the two subjects that yield the highest average income. If you can excel in one or both of these areas, then there is a good chance that you will do well in

---

[1] "Child Development Tracker." PBS, N.d. Web. < http://www.pbs.org/ parents/ child-development/>.

college and in your career. To properly motivate a child to do well in these areas, it would certainly help to start working with them during their most critical years of development.

After reading through this site, my suspicions were confirmed. Moreover, significant development starts instantaneously after birth. Before the age of two, children can learn the difference between *one* and *two*. They understand the basic idea of singular versus plural. Measurements and depth have some appreciation as shown by grasping for objects as well as filling and emptying different containers. Children also get a feeling for sequence as they fall into their daily routines and naptimes. From a scientific standpoint, they learn to use their senses and the difference between light and dark. Infants and very young children love to explore and learn about the feel and movement of different objects. This is shown through their propensity to splash, squeeze, and bang on various objects.

As children move closer to three years old, they really focus on the trial and error method. They can take simple directions and start to pretend more when they play. This is significant because they can now pretend that an object now stands for something else; a precursor to their later battles with algebra. Their sense of exploration and wonder is now heightened by their ability to move and improvement of motor skills. They also notice how other objects move. This is the time when children first start to categorize things.

As a child approaches four, he or she can start to solve simple puzzles and recognize written numbers. They start to master their descriptions and labels for their surroundings. They can count and even start adding and subtracting to a degree. Children are also now starting to become aware of physics. They understand that water will drain and that gravity exists. The growing language at this age is instrumental to their learning. They are full of questions and absorb everything with which they come into contact.

We are now moving to the age where it is critical to correctly stimulate a child. Most initial learning is natural, but children start to define the path their lives will ultimately take at this young age. If the parent does not feed the hunger that is there, a child can easily fall out of track when compared to a child raised by a more attentive parent.Knowing this makes me wish that I had been paired with Jermaine earlier.

As children move closer to age five,they now know the concept of time, but may have trouble telling time. They do know the months of the year and days of the week though. A child's counting is also becoming more crisp and accurate. They can really delve into more complex word problems and work through them to find a solution. Descriptions become more accurate and refined. Children can also start to use instruments like rulers and thermometers and they are more aware of the weather.

As children start school, their imaginations are running wild and they are beginning to use compound sentences. Children can now participate in class, but learn to speak in turn. They are starting to paint, read, and write. The world is opening up and they are getting hands-on experience. The arts are also starting to pique their interests as children can begin to show aptitude for music and short plays. They are learning through conversation and points can be amplified by pictures and graphs.

A child at this age has hit the point of no return. He or she will keep up with classmates or fall behind. Once a child falls behind, they are more prone to being satisfied with that lag and may never catch back up to his or her peers. Most people would not worry about the future of a five-year-old, but this is a critical age for development. The subject matter in school is getting more complicated. Soon, students will be expected to read at an increasing level as well as continually improve their handwriting. Parents are vital to this growth. Children with better parents will flourish and children with lesser parents will struggle.Progression is enhanced by practicing at home.

The Center for Disease Control (CDC) has also conducted studies on this subject. They found that students with proactive parents make higher test scores, have better behavior and better social skills [2]. Furthermore, they are less likely to smoke cigarettes, drink alcohol, and become pregnant. These children also tend to be more physically active. The fact is that attentive parents create better children and ultimately make functional adults. It is a monumental disadvantage to be the child of an unprepared parent.

Why are the teachers unable to pick up the slack left by the parents? A considerable amount of tax dollars go toward education. Should we expect this investment to fall flat for some students? Well, let us consider the facts. Budgets are consistently shrinking for education. Tax payers are reproducing at a lower rate than non-taxpayers

---

[2] "Child Development." Centers for Disease Control and Prevention. N.p., 19 Nov. 2013. Web. <http://www.cdc.gov/ncbddd/childdevelopment/index.html>.

and that is creating a situation where there are more kids being taught using less dollars. This causes more crowded class rooms and less one-on-one attention between the student and teacher.

Furthermore, not all teachers are great at their jobs. Teaching is hard. In many cases, it is difficult to make it through the day when only dealing with the disciplinary concerns of a classroom. Fewer teachers can focus on shaping young minds as their role has become a hybrid between instructing and babysitting. It is a tough commentary to write, but an unavoidable truth.

Barbara Nemko and Harold Kwalwasser did a study for the *Wall Street Journal* which found that the admissions and graduation standards of many colleges of education are extremely low [3]. To further illustrate that point, Rita Kramer wrote a book entitled *Ed School Follies: The Miseducation of America's Teachers.* She discovered that teachers were generally well-versed in teaching theory and presentation, but had a poor understanding of the actual subject matter.

Nemko and Kwalwasser found, once again, that the subject of math reared its head. Education students had a lower average SAT math score of 486 when compared to the average for all freshmen of 516. The reality is that teachers are learning how to teach, but getting a meager diet when it comes to the material that needs to be presented. The authors' solution to this problem is quite obvious. Do not allow prospective teachers to major in education. Make them learn an actual discipline, major in it, and then teach it.

As I mentioned before, teaching is an enormous responsibility and an even more difficult occupation. I am not belittling anyone that makes that career choice because I am well aware of the challenge. With that said, it is evident that not every teacher is up to the task. When you combine that issue with a lax curriculum that comes from many education colleges, it is clear that there is a flaw in relying on teachers for 100% of a child's academic growth. Parents must supplement that effort. Many teachers do everything that they can for a student, but they still need parental assistance, and a lot of it.

Conversely, studies are showing that teachers are struggling with their relationships with their students' parents. Galaxy Research surveyed 816 primary and secondary teachers and uncovered some

[3] Nemko, Barbara, and Harold Kwalwasser. "Why Teacher Colleges Get a Flunking Grade." The Wall Street Journal. N.p., N.d. Web. 23 Oct. 2013.

alarming trends [4][5]. Half of the teachers in this study had been verbally abused by a parent. Sixty percent of the teachers said that children do not give them the proper respect. This is an amazing statement when I consider my school experience. If I was ever disrespectful to a teacher, it was bad news when I got home. Punishment of some sort was imminent and it would certainly be more severe than anything that would be handed out by the school.

A teacher commenting about the lack of discipline and support from parents was a consistent theme of the survey. Teachers cannot control what happens outside of school hours, but may be expected to clean up the mess during the brief window of time they have with a student each day.Bullying is also become a more severe problem because of a lack of parental monitoring in the home. Due to social media, cyber-bullying is increasing and that adds another element that is taking away from productive class time.

Parents are frequently taking a back seat in education and if they do take a side in the parent versus student debate, they often take the side of the student. Ron Clark wrote an article for CNN titled *What Teachers Really Want to Tell Parents* [6]. He found that the average teaching career is less than five years in length. Rather than blaming the students, poor parenting is the reason given by most teachers who leave the job early. Parents have trouble taking a teacher at their word. They seem to think that the instructor has some kind of agenda against their "precious snowflake" rather than actually working with them to correct the behavior.

The article continues to outline many other problems that teachers deal with on a frequent basis when interacting with parents. Bad grades are taken personally. Parents start to equate good grades with good teaching. However, many times, teachers give good grades just to avoid conflicts with parents. The truly great educators give appropriate grades because that system is the only way for a student to improve in the areas where they are weak. Clark went on to say that more and more parents are actually bringing lawyers to their teacher meetings.

---

[4] Kramer, Rita. "Ed School Follies: The Miseducation of America's Teachers." IUniverse, 2 Jan. 2001. Web.

[5] Barry, Evonne. "We've Had Enough, It's Time to Raise Your Own Kids, Teachers Say." NewsComAu. N.p., 30 Jan. 2012. Web.

[6] Clark, Ron. "What Teachers Really Want to Tell Parents." CNN. Cable News Network, 14 Mar. 2013. Web.

One final point made by the article is that teachers are now worrying about their job safety because of the wrath of parents. Mr. Clark illustrates a story where a teacher marked on a child's face with a permanent marker. It was a mistake and she tried to clean off the mark. The parent was furious and the teacher ultimately lost her job.

I have a close friend with a similar story.Luke (the policeman I mentioned earlier) and I have been friends for a long time. I moved before my junior year of high school to Franklin, TN. Luke was the only other guy in my class that took honors classes and played football. Because of those two factors, we were destined to spend a lot of time together. We have a lot in common and it was great to have a friend that shared the same academic and athletic challenges. Luke was an English major in college and got his teaching credential for the state of Tennessee by getting a master's degree. He wanted to teach.

New teachers do not typically get the best classes. Oddly, the more experienced educators are assigned to the better behaved and more gifted classrooms. One would think that the more seasoned veterans would have the task of working with the more challenging classrooms. However, that is not typically the case. Generally, as teachers serve their time, they are rewarded by being allowed to work with the *better* children.

Luke fell into this predicament as he was assigned to one of the more problematic classes at his new job in Birmingham, AL. I heard story after story from him about how little the students cared and this was reinforced by disinterested parents. Once again, more involved parents were the key to better students. He was yelled at by students and parents. Grades were poor and expecting homework to be turned in was a pipedream.

With that said, Luke and I were not always a joy to have in class. We both made excellent grades (his were better than mine). However, under the veil of being an honor student we would fall out of line on occasion in class. We would both challenge teachers and lived to contradict items that were taught as fact or were printed in the book. Luke and I were separated in a few classes to try to make the hour pass more smoothly. It is difficult to call a parent meeting when your complaint about a child is that he or she is critically thinking–*and we knew that.*

Maybe teaching this type of class was Luke's penance for making life difficult for his grade school teachers. Still, his teaching career did not last long. He had a student shove him in class. Luke responded by sending the child into the hall and having another student fetch the principal. While in the hallway, the student took a swing at him. Luke, who is a big guy (also wrestled in high school), pinned the teenager to the wall and waited for the principal to show. At this point the student was escorted to the principal's office and Luke went back to teaching his class.

A few weeks later he was asked to resign over the incident. The child's mother was furious that her son had been physically handled. It did not matter that he had assaulted a teacher twice. At this point, Luke had acquiesced to the fact that teaching was not going to be his calling. He calmly asked, "What should I have done in that situation?" The alternative seemed to be to simply let the child throw punches until he tired. The principal said that he should have backed away and asked the child, "What are you doing?"

My friend is now much happier being a police officer in Nashville. He is a brilliant guy and destroyed the police academy academic records. Luke missed one question on a test and was perfect on the rest. This mark may never be broken. I imagine that he would have been a great teacher, but I am glad that he has found an occupation that interests him. This was another story of a promising educator having their career cut short because of poor parenting.

We want great teachers and we want to provide our children with a top-notch education. However, we are not doing the things that are necessary to make that happen. Teachers are being pushed to generic education degrees and frequently struggle with mastery of the very subjects they are teaching. We are also forcing our best teachers to move to other occupations because it is not worth the headache for them to deal with awful students and parents on a daily basis.

All parents will flippantly say that they want what is best for their children. It is an ingrained response and they are quick to draw it from the holster. Through ignorance or laziness, their actions are not backing the assertion. Parents need to wait until they are financially and emotionally mature before they have children. Then, they have to proactively stay involved in the development of a child. It is a massive commitment, but a necessary one if that young person is going to develop into a self-sustaining adult.

Teachers cannot do it alone and we need to give them all of the support we can. The trends inherent from cyclical poverty and from the diminished attraction of the teaching profession are troubling. At some point, it is possible that wealthier parents will want to permanently separate their children and send them to private schools while more working class families may choose to homeschool. Public schools will spiral right along with generational poverty and fall in their effectiveness to educate with every passing year. This is a very real crisis and, unfortunately, additional money cannot fix the problem.

Chapter 15

Nashville Gang Life

When I heard about the shooting, I could not believe that Chastity could make such an irresponsible decision. Dating a gang member is not only ill-advised, but incredibly dangerous. She also exercised poor judgment when deciding to drive her boyfriend's car after he was incarcerated. The shooting was quite an awakening for me about the gang culture in the Nashville area. I thought that gangs were reserved for larger cities like Chicago and Los Angeles.

As I continued to work with Jermaine, I found that gangs were a real threat in his community. GangFree.org lists the following reasons that a young person would join a gang [1]:

1. Lack of jobs for youth
2. Poverty compounded by social isolation
3. Domestic violence
4. Negative peer networks
5. Lack of parental supervision
6. Early academic failure and lack of school attachment

We have already covered many of these subjects. The website continues with some more complex ideas about why someone might join a gang. Gangs provide a sense of family. If an adolescent is not getting the connection they seek from his or her parents, they are prone to look for it somewhere else. Gang life is also an alternative for someone that is being abused at home. It provides them with protection and with a unique level of discipline. They are now expected to do certain things and are held accountable for the results.

Gangs have evolved and many are a traditional part of the community. Someone might join a gang because they have family members in it. There is enormous peer pressure to be a part of the gang and

[1] "Why People Join Gangs." Gangfree.org, N.d. Web. <http://www.gangfree.org/gangs_why.html>.

it provides a young man or woman with a sense of purpose and respect. Their new life is much more exciting than going to school or staying at home all day. It also gives them a consistent means to make money. Children that take this path are starting to find an identity within this group.

The crimes that gangs commit cover two basic elements: wanting to be seen and wanting to make money.Signs with their hands, colors, graffiti, and tattoos are all used to get attention. I was sincerely worried about Jermaine getting tattooed at 16 years old. There was a definite risk that he could be entering a gang and this was part of that initiation. I do not believe that it was, but his family does have some gang ties. These different elements are seen as a way to better one's self and take the place of hard work, education, and saving.

The site also gives advice for parents if they suspect that their child might be interested in joining a gang. They encourage parents to explain risky behavior they have experienced and share what they have learned from their mistakes. Parents should take a strong stance that gang life is unacceptable and start explaining their rules while the child is young; put a high value on education and praise the types of behaviors that are beneficial in a child's development. They also say that parents must stay involved. They need to know their children's friends and be a positive example.

My first encounter with a gang in Nashville came from playing softball. I typically play at a field that is in a dicey part of the city. It does not quite rival the area where Jermaine lives in northeast Nashville, but this southeast area of town is not great either. This part of Nashville is home to many low-income families. Some are immigrants and others are older people that have lived there a long time and simply had the area change around them.

The prevalent gang in this part of town is actually Kurdish. A 2007 *New York Times* article entitled *Street gang emerges from Kurdish community in Nashville* explains that Kurds started to flee Iraq in the 1970s after the collapse of an autonomy movement [2]. Kurdish people share a common language and homeland. Kurdistan is the term for an area that branches through the countries of Iraq, Turkey, Syria, and Iran. As the war-torn area produced more refugees, they started to move to the same part of Middle Tennessee as those that

[2] Emery, Theo. "Street Gang Emerges from Kurdish Community in Nashville." New York Times, 15 July 2007. Web.

had left earlier. Gradually, the Kurdish community started to form in Nashville and is the biggest collection of Kurds in the country.

The author, Theo Emery, further explains that the community has now more than 8,000 people.Around the year 2000, a gang started to form. Some of the younger Kurds began to call themselves "Kurdish Pride" (or KP). They have many of the characteristics of a traditional gang. They use yellow as a common color and have tattoos even though tattoos are explicitly forbidden by Islam. Many in the Kurdish community are becoming aware of the gang and the potential effect they are having on their reputation.

Their concern is warranted because the gang has become more brazen and is involved in many illegal activities. KP members have been found guilty of rape, burglary, and even murder. The gang received its most serious attention after four members were arrested for conspiracy of first-degree murder against a police officer. This policeman was targeted for breaking up a drug deal.

The Nashville Metropolitan Police Force decided to take a page out of the gang-stopping handbook used by Los Angeles. A Vocativ.com article entitled *The Rise and Fall of Kurdish Gangs in Nashville* explains that local law enforcement started to use an injunction against the gang and its known members [3]. The most effective part of the injunction was to pinpoint a part of Nashville that was off-limits to the gang. The ACLU has expressed concerns over this method of gang prevention saying that it violates the civil rights of the members. Still, the 1.5 mile area that was partitioned has been instrumental in limiting KP crime.

In the middle of that gang-free zone is Paragon Mills Park. One day I walked to the field to start a softball game and saw a considerable amount of gang graffiti by KP. There is a clubhouse at the front of the park that was completely covered. In addition, light poles, park benches, fences, and different parts of the parking lot had traces of graffiti. It was quite a site. The park has never felt completely safe. During the many years I have played ball there, I have heard a variety of gunshots. The worst crime I can recall is hearing about a man that was stripped and beaten over twenty dollars. His nearly lifeless, naked body was left under a car.

Today the park is much safer for a variety of reasons. It is patrolled at night by a police officer. He will literally sit in his squad car in

[3]Cavaliere, Victoria. "The Rise and Fall of Kurdish Gangs in Nashville." Vocative, 20 Nov. 2013. Web.

the parking lot and make sure that we make it safely to our cars. Furthermore, the injunction worked. The gang has basically been dismantled and their activity has no medium to conduct business. According to this article, Charlotte, Orlando, and even London have had success with partitioning gang areas. Chicago and New York have had less success as human rights groups have shot down the injunctions before they could be put into place.

The two prevailing gangs of Nashville are the better-known Crips and Bloods. A newspaper out of Memphis, *The Commercial Appeal*, had an article entitled *Big 4: Gangster Disciples, Vice Lords, Crips, Bloods* which gives some basic details on the two major gangs [4]. Crips use the color blue and were founded in 1969 in Los Angeles. They can also use some black and purple. It is common to see them use sports teams to fly their colors. Common teams include the Los Angeles Lakers and Dodgers as well as the Kansas City Royals. They typically use the three-point crown and grapes as an identifying symbol.

According to the article, the Bloods appeared a year or two later in Los Angeles. Their main color is red and they avoid the color blue as well as the letter “C” because of their longstanding rivalry with the Crips. They commonly wear Budweiser NASCAR racing clothing and use a five-point crown as their symbol. Bloods tend to use dogs in their tattoos as well. The gang has a more defined hierarchy and ranking system while the Crips are less formal.

The local news station, New Channel 2 did a series on area gangs. *News 2 Extra: Gangs in Middle Tennessee* points out that the Nashville rivalry between the Bloods and the Crips has been going strong for over two decades [5]. The series identifies how the gang culture is engrained into the city's culture. The two gangs are highly involved in making money through selling narcotics and weapons as well as invading homes. They are involved in serious crime and they start recruiting at an early age. The News Channel 2 series leaned on the expertise of one of Metro's gang unit members, Sergeant Gary Kemper. He commented that kids join gangs in the fifth or sixth grade and rarely change course to a legal lifestyle.

Not only was I incorrect in my assumption that Nashville lacked gangs, but I had no clue about the level in which they operate. In my

[4] "Big 4: Gangster Disciples, Vice Lords, Crips, Bloods." The Commercial Appeal, 23 Mar. 2008. Web.

[5] "News 2 Extra: Gangs in Middle Tennessee." WKRN News 2, 11 Nov. 2009. Web.

research I found many stories about serious gang crime taking place in Nashville.The *Lebanon Democrat* did a story on a gang member named Ray Moody in late 2013 [6]. He was found guilty of cooking crack-cocaine as well as possession of multiple weapons in his residence. Among the weapons found was a semi-automatic compact firearm.

Moody spent about a year in jail in 2009 for different charges by the state. However, during this time, his girlfriend took care of his weapon and drug stash. When released, he went back to drug trafficking at the exact same residence. His latest 2011 arrest was the most serious. With his history as a convicted felon, it is illegal to be found with guns and ammunition. Moody was found in 2011 with shotgun shells and more crack-cocaine. He faces a long prison sentence that could possibly end up being a life sentence.

The most troubling part of gang life in this area is the concentration of violence within the African-American *community*. Erik Avanier of WDEF News 12 in Chattanooga did a report called *Black on black crime hurting Chattanooga's African American* community [7]. The report estimates that almost 90% of gang members in the Chattanooga area are black. Avanier also comments on many of the same topics that we have already examined. Black teens are facing situations where they have poor support at home and limited job prospects when they come of age. Furthermore, the problem is exacerbated if they do get incarcerated. It becomes even more difficult to find work and more likely that former inmates will revert back to gang life.

According to the Violence Policy Center, in 2008 Nashville had the fifth-highest rate of black homicides in the country [8]. Brian Haas of *The Tennessean* wrote an article entitled *Black Homicides Reach "Crisis" in Nashville* [9]. He mentions the 42 murders that took place in 2008 as well as the fact that the homicide rate continued to rise the following year. Haas states that in "Nashville if you are African-American, you are four to five times more likely to be murdered than

[6]"Nashville Gang Member Convicted of Drug Trafficking, Firearms Offenses near Elementary School." Lebanon Democrat. N.p., 26 Nov. 2013. Web.

[7]Avanier, Erik. "Black on Black Crime Hurting Chattanooga's African American Community." WDEF News 12, N.d. Web.

[8]Wallace, Hunter. "Black Run America: Black Homicides Reach "Crisis Level" in Nashville." Occidental Dissent. Occidental Dissent, 14 Apr. 2011. Web.

[9]Haas, Brian. "Black Homicides Reach "Crisis" in Nashville." The Tennessean, N.d. Web.

if you are white." Not all murders are gang related, but most stem from the same basic problem in the black community—*hopelessness.*

The poverty level among Nashville's black community is substantial. The article states that "Nashville's black residents are almost twice as likely to have incomes below the poverty level, 2009 census data show. The average African-American family of four with two children brought in less than $22,000 a year." The direct correlation between poverty and crime is staggering. As you move up the socioeconomic ladder, violent crime becomes less and less frequent.

One anecdote that caught my eye in the article revolves around the deceased Christopher Evans. He was shot dead at age 16 on November 26, 2008. His mother, Kim Maupin, knew that he was struggling with depression and smoked pot. At age 16, he had also joined a gang. She claims to have asked a judge to lock him up because she knew what his fate would be. Christopher left behind a two-year-old daughter.

To counter the growing gang problem in Nashville, Metro Police formed a gang unit in 2003. In addition to this new focus on gang activity, Nashville schools are joining in the effort with a more proactive approach. Judith R. Tackett of GangWar.com mentions programs such as

> "S.T.A.R.'s (Students Taking A Right Stand), the Path Program, the Second Step Program, and some bullying programs that target students from elementary to high school."[10]

In addition to these measures, schools are now conducting regular searches.

Gang activity also affects the innocent people that live in the area. Like Tremaine and Chastity, there are numerous stories of bystanders being shot as a result of collateral damage during a gang shooting. Haas mentions a couple of other Nashville victims of this kind of crime. They can be young and old. Anyone living in project housing is at risk. With limited opportunities and a need for safeguarding, it is easy to understand how a youth can be led into gang life.

Metro Councilman Jerry Maynard commented[11] that:

---

[10]Tackett, Judith R. "Gangs Infiltrate Virtually Every High School." STARS. N.p., 19 Jan. 2006. Web. <http://www.studentstakingarightstand.org/news.htm>.

[11]Tackett, Judith R. "Gangs Infiltrate Virtually Every High School." STARS. N.p., 19 Jan. 2006. Web. <http://www.studentstakingarightstand.org/news.htm>.

> "black-on-black crime is not a black problem . It's a Nashville problem because tourists will not come here, businesses will not come here. We will strangle economic growth if we do not come to a solution to this."

There are various stories of small groups and individuals that are genuinely trying to make a difference in that community. Still, the recurrent stated problem is the exposure that young children have to mature subject matter. They see violence, prostitution, and drugs at such an early age that they take these vices to be normal elements of everyday life.

I do not see the spillover happening to quite the degree that Mr. Maynard describes. However, there will be increased costs to the taxpayer through added welfare and prison expansion. Gang growth is a real challenge for impoverished communities. Shifting the idea of *opportunity* from a life of violence to a life of education and a life dedicated to working up a career ladder is difficult. Finding a way to accomplish this change in mindset will be critical for the lower-income segments of the community.

Chapter 16

The Curse of Uncle Tom

Uncle Tom is the primary character from Harriet Beecher Stowe's 1852 novel, *Uncle Tom's Cabin.* According to Claire Parfait, who wrote, *The Publishing History of Uncle Tom's Cabin,* Stowe was furious about the new Fugitive Slave Act of 1850 and wrote this book as a response [1]. This legislation required northern assistance in an effort to return escaped slaves to their owners. Noncompliance could result in a $1,000 fine or imprisonment.

Parfait further explains that Stowe got the idea for her novel because of the circumstances surrounding a slave named Josiah Henson. Josiah was born into slavery in 1789 and became a Christian when he was 18 years old. He was promised by his owner that he could buy his freedom for $450. Josiah was able to raise $350 and secured a promissory note for the remaining amount. When he confronted his owner to take him up on his offer, the price was raised to $1,000.

Henson was unable to counter his double-cross. It was impossible for him to prove the original deal existed—not that anyone would listen to a slave anyway. Josiah contemplated killing his owner and even managed to procure a gun. However, due to his Christian beliefs he abstained. Josiah Henson would later escape with his family to Canada where he would become a civic leader. Some believe that Stowe met Henson at one time, but that has never been proven.

Stowe's story has a more heartbreaking tone and conclusion than Josiah's tale. Uncle Tom is a similar man though. He is principled and kind. He does everything that is asked of him by the slave owners and can handle unbelievable amounts of work. Uncle Tom's story would come to an end when he refused to reveal information about a couple of female slaves that had escaped. Even after his relentless effort and status as a *good slave,* Uncle Tom is beaten to death by his cruel master.

This story was obviously controversial during the time in which it was written. According to Sarah Meer, who wrote *Uncle Tom Mania:*

[1] Parfait, Claire. "The Publishing History of Uncle Tom's Cabin." Ashgate, 23 Nov. 2007. Web.

Slavery, Minstrelsy, and Transatlantic Culture in the 1850s, Senator Charles Sumner credited Stowe's novel as the reason that Abraham Lincoln was elected [2]. Meer further explained that Lincoln actually made a remark about the novel starting the American Civil War. Frederick Douglas called the book, "a flash to light a million camp fires in front of the embattled hosts of slavery."

Not everyone accepted the Uncle Tom character or Stowe's novel within the civil rights and African-American communities. In 2004, Deborah J. Rosenthal came across this quote from an anonymous reviewer for *The Liberator* [3]:

> "Uncle Tom's character is sketched with great power and rare religious perception. It triumphantly exemplifies the nature, tendency, and results of Christian non-resistance. We are curious to know whether Mrs. Stowe is a believer in the duty of non-resistance for the White man, under all possible outrage and peril, as for the Black man... [For whites in parallel circumstances, it is often said] Talk not of overcoming evil with good—it is madness! Talk not of peacefully submitting to chains and stripes—it is base servility! Talk not of servants being obedient to their masters—let the blood of tyrants flow! How is this to be explained or reconciled? Is there one law of submission and non-resistance for the Black man, and another of rebellion and conflict for the white man? When it is the whites who are trodden in the dust, does Christ justify them in taking up arms to vindicate their rights? And when it is the blacks who are thus treated, does Christ require them to be patient, harmless, long-suffering, and forgiving? Are there two Christs?"

James Weldon Johnson wrote in his book, *The Autobiography of an Ex Colored Man* [4]:

> "For my part, I was never an admirer of Uncle Tom, nor of his type of goodness; but I believe that there were lots of old Negroes as foolishly good as he; the proof of which is that they knowingly stayed and

[2] Meer, Sarah. "Uncle Tom Mania: Slavery, Minstrelsy, and Transatlantic Culture in the 1850s." University of Georgia, 1 Apr. 2005. Web.

[3] Rosenthal, Deborah J. "A Rutledge Literary Sourcebook on Harriet Beecher Stowe's Uncle Tom's Cabin." Rutledge, 2004. Web.

[4] Johnson, James Weldon. "The Autobiography of an Ex-Colored Man." Dover Publications, 10 May 1995. Web.

> worked on the plantations that furnished sinews for the army which was fighting to keep them enslaved."

Although not the intent, Harriet Beecher Stowe had created a character that would evolve to represent a willing servant; someone that was too obedient to rise above his oppressors. The *Urban Dictionary* defines an "Uncle Tom" as "A black man who will do anything to stay in good standing with 'the white man' including betray his own people [5]."

My first experience with this derogatory usage came while I was in high school. My honors classes generally contained the same group of students with an occasional exception (a student may take Honors English and U.S. History, but not take Honors Physics for example). Among that group was one black student and she was a beautiful and brilliant young woman. She did well in her classes and was always well dressed and neatly organized. She was a model student.

For her appearance and acumen in the classroom, she started being called "Uncle Tom" by some of the other black students. I picked up on this in the football locker room (sports are the great melting-pot for high school students). Somehow, wearing newer clothing and making good grades meant that she was trying to act "white" or show subservience to white people. I know that it bothered her.

Occasionally, she would come to school with a more "black" look. Instead of her normal dress or sweater, she would wear a sports jersey or something else that was out of the ordinary. She was attempting to fit in with the other black students while continuing her more rigorous studies among a class of white students. It was a difficult situation for her to navigate.

I regret that I have not kept up with her after graduation, but I know she took an academic scholarship to a prestigious ACC school.

The idea of "subservience by choice" is a very real issue with many people in the black community. It is so important to be defiant that they are willing to sacrifice their educations and even their careers. Chastity has had this problem from time to time when she would work. I mentioned the incident that occurred while she worked at a local grocery store. Chastity was upset with her boss after being

[5] Kimdigity. "Uncle Tom." Urban Dictionary, 10 June 2003. Web. <http://www.urbandictionary.com/define.php?term=Uncle%20Tom>.

asked to do something out of the ordinary. She felt that her boss was being disrespectful and decided to be rude in return. Chastity was asked to leave as a result.

In 2008, NPR interviewed folklorist Patricia Turner on the subject. She remarks that the African-American community does not hate the actual Uncle Tom character. However, they despise the distorted version of this character that has evolved over time [6]. Uncle Tom was intended to be a strong, Christian man that gave his life to save two others. Over time, he became a sellout. He is now seen as an older man with poor English who will do anything to appease his white oppressors. There may not be a greater insult to a black person than to call him or her an "Uncle Tom."

Turner continued by explaining that *Uncle Tom's Cabin* was more popular than the *Bible* when it was first published. However, the evolution of Uncle Tom into a subservient sellout started on stage. Producers felt that they could sell more tickets by depicting Uncle Tom in a way that was more popular in that time. At the time Blacks were often portrayed as dancing imbeciles that would completely roll-over at the request of their white masters. Furthermore, the ending of the tale was usually changed from Uncle Tom being beaten to death to a completely opposite conclusion. At the request of his white oppressors, he gives up the location of the escapees.

For fear of being called "Uncle Tom," many in the black community feel forced to conform to a certain set of rules. First and foremost, African-Americans are expected to be Democrats (as discussed in Chapter 11). Scott Jaschik of InsideHigherEd.com did a story about a fired college professor named Jean R. Cobbs. Cobbs is described as an outspoken, black, Republican woman [7]. She worked at Virginia State University, which is a historically black college. This environment created a unique situation for her and certainly left her in the political minority when compared to her colleagues.

VSU violated their own methods of due process and fired Jean Cobbs. She was a tenured professor and had 33 years of service to the school. Cobbs was a sociology and social work professor and claimed that the defamation had started about 12 years before she was ultimately

[6]Turner, Patricia. "Why *African-Americans* Loathe 'Uncle Tom'" NPR, 30 July 2008. Web.

[7]Jaschik, Scott. "$600K for Fired Professor." InsideHigherEd.com, 26 Jan. 2007. Web.

fired. With an impending discrimination suit surfacing, VSU agreed to pay $600,000 to her.

Jean Cobbs now works as a volunteer at a home for at-risk children. Jaschik asked her about returning to her job, but she had no interest. With the same administration that had fired her still in place, she said, "There's not much for me to go back to." She concluded the interview by saying, "When this kind of injustice goes on for years, your career is ruined, and the only thing you can try to do is be vindicated," she said. "I hope this will make it better for other individuals."

In 2002, M.A. Knight wrote an article for FrontPageMag.com. He details some of the issues that an African-American might have when talking about being conservative [8]. His article is entitled *Are Black Conservatives "Uncle Toms"? Yes ....* He refers to Professor Cobbs' story, but has quite a story of his own. He recalls a political conversation that he had with some of his black colleagues. He mentioned that he, a black man himself, had voted for a Republican candidate. The group was so disgusted with him that they called him all kinds of names and eventually turned and walked away from him. One even spat at his feet!

He then recalls getting on the bus to go home from work the next day. The person that had spat at him was waiting as well and Knight expected trouble from the impending encounter. As he approached, the man confessed something that completely surprised Knight: he admitted that he was also a Republican. Naturally, Mr. Knight asked him why he did not stand up for him. The man responded, "I have to work with these guys everyday, y'know."

The author gives a couple of reasons why he believes that black conservatives are sellouts, but they are not the reasons that you might expect:

> (1) "Because we have consistently failed to protect and defend our own. When brave souls such as Kay James, Alan Keyes, Condi Rice, Clarence Thomas, Thomas Sowell, JC Watts, etc. are attacked, where is our outrage? And if indeed we are outraged, how come the entire world doesn't know about it? When we are called names, why do we not fight back and make sure that person would think a VERY long time about it before he/she does it again? If we cannot stand up for ourselves, why would anyone respect us enough to listen to us? Is it

[8] Knight, M. A. "Are Black Conservatives "Uncle Toms"? Yes..." FrontPageMag.com, 10 Dec. 2002. Web.

> a wonder then, that our arguments are simply dismissed and we are just called names instead of being civilly debated against? Challenging the name calling and innuendo directed against us black Conservatives is not only a matter of justice, it would serve to open people's minds and thus yield dividends for us in terms of effectively taking our message to the black community. This I can personally attest to.
>
> (2) Because we have not taken our message to our people. If we truly believed that Conservative principles would help our communities best and that the grip the Left has on the black community is destroying us, then our virtual silence is unconscionable. As black Conservatives, no one is more an advocate of self-help and raising ourselves by our bootstraps. But on this issue, we've done an extremely pathetic job of living up to our own principles."

This issue within the black community reminds me of the way that white people would behave when confronted with the subject of slavery in the 1800s. The *good whites* would say that they were upset about its abolishment. However, whites that spoke out against slavery were putting themselves in harm's way when speaking out within their own community. This was an issue where it was not okay to have a different opinion. Many white people were beaten and killed because of their stance against slavery. In this case, they were the sellouts and they were the Uncle Toms.

The remainder of the article takes more of a slant on how to spread the conservative message throughout the black community. Still, Mr. Knight's point is that understanding is the key to acceptance.He told another story about a white, conservative politician winning an election in a historically minority-driven district. The candidate's message of lowered taxes and a strengthened community worked and he won. To that point, hard work and education is a message that needs to be spread. If it is not culturally acceptable to be successful this way, then this adds a whole new dimension to the challenge of pulling a community out of poverty.

This battle within the black community is not only reserved to the more impoverished areas. Garry Cobb wrote an article in 2011 that can be found on GCobb.com on the subject. In *Jalen Rose Calls Grant Hill An Uncle Tom For Growing Up In Two-Parent Family,* he leads the article by talking about the Uncle Tom problem in his own life [9]. He recounts:

---

[9] Cobb, Garry. "Jalen Rose Calls Grant Hill An Uncle Tom For Growing Up In Two-Parent Family." GCobb.com, 17 Mar. 2011. Web.

> "My Dad forced all of my brothers and sisters to do well in school, but I hated it because of some of the other black kids in the school would call me an "Uncle Tom" behind my back because I did my work and didn't get in trouble. Many of the black kids who went to my high school did bad on purpose because it wasn't cool to do well in school, if you were black."

The story itself centers on Jalen Rose. Rose was a member of the University of Michigan's *Fab Five* basketball team from the early '90s. This team embodied the *right way* of being successful for much of the African-American community. Cobb explains that the team was brash, had stylish haircuts, wore black socks, and had baggy shorts that are now common in the NBA. They were the acceptable format for success because they did not conform to the normal rules. It was not enough to be great at the sport, they had to do it in a way that directly clashed with society's norms.

In an ESPN documentary on the *Fab Five*, Rose talks about the Uncle Tom issue further and even pinpoints another NBA player, Grant Hill. Hill played for Duke University and that team was the model for college basketball excellence. They were clean-cut and well disciplined. Grant Hill, in Rose's eyes, was a traitor because he played for Duke. He further explained that Duke did not recruit players like Rose. He was incredibly talented, but came from a broken home. He further explains that:

> "I felt that they only recruited black players that were Uncle Toms. ... I was jealous of Grant Hill. He came from a great black family. Congratulations. Your mom went to college and was roommates with Hillary Clinton. Your dad played in the NFL as a very well-spoken and successful man. I was upset and bitter that my mom had to bust her hump for 20-plus years. I was bitter that I had a professional athlete that was my father that I didn't know. I resented that, moreso than I resented him. I looked at it as they are who the world accepts and we are who the world hates."

Garry Cobb does an exceptional job of explaining this issue:

> "Rose voiced a sentiment that is found frequently in the black community. Many times African-Americans who try to live successful lives

> are hated and chastised by those of their own race. Rose's comments pulled the cover off of some of the poisonous attitudes which are dooming African-American youngsters who grow up without their Dads, intentionally shun education, get in trouble with the law and go on to live their lives in poverty amongst crime and ruin."

Grant Hill was an "Uncle Tom" because he had it easier than many other black people. His parents were married and well-educated. Cobb explains that the critical issue plaguing many black children is that their fathers are not a part of their lives. The author states that 70% of African-American children are born out of wedlock. Grant Hill is the minority in this demographic and Rose, as well as many other blacks, resent him for that.

Mr. Cobb's story is similar to Grant Hill's. He played in the NFL and his father was a star in the locker room. His African-American teammates were amazed at the relationship that a black man could have with his father. Cobb explains that his father was instrumental in his growth as a man and was the biggest influence in his life.

The article continues to hit several key problems that arise from the Uncle Tom mentality. Many African-Americans despise Grant Hill's success. While Rose's Michigan basketball team was wildly popular in the black community, Hill was never embraced in the same way. Cobb also mentions that Donovan McNabb had a similar fate with his popularity. He was an extremely successful black quarterback, but was never extraordinarily popular. The author believes that this is a direct result of his stable upbringing through a two-parent home.

It is easier for much of the black community to identify with players that have a troubled past. The author uses Michael Vick as an example. He is still wildly popular even after his jail stint for dog fighting. He may even be more popular now than he was before that incident. My wife's family is all Atlanta Falcons fans and I will attend an occasional Falcons' game. It is still common to see a Vick jersey. It does not matter that he killed dogs or that he no longer plays with the team. Many in the black community can identify with a man that has had a troubled past and love the fact that he is still successful.The remainder of the article is more of a religious argument, but he does hit on a couple of key problems. If a community is taught to have poisonous attitudes, then they are going to have priorities in place that lead to failure. Cobb sites a few different examples of these detrimental themes: Children are supposed to come from a one-parent home. It is frowned upon to stay out of trouble and policemen are seen as the enemy. Drug dealers are seen as heroes and sexual promiscuity is the mark of a real man. Having children at a young age is the sign of a desirable woman.These common beliefs are a poison within the African-American and many poor communites and a consistent reason that there are not more Grant Hills in the world.

Vince Mancini wrote an article called *Tyler Perry says Spike Lee can go to hell* where he discusses the feud between the two [10]. Both are extremely successful filmmakers, but their genres and styles are very different. Spike Lee uses a more acceptable style. His movies are graphic with high levels of violence, nudity, and language. He makes movies that are more controversial and less appealing to the masses. Tyler Perry's movies are a stark contrast because they make fun of black stereotypes and are more family friendly. Spike Lee has accused Perry of being an Uncle Tom because he accuses him of catering to the masses to make money. He is a sellout. On the eve of the release of Perry's movie, *Medea*, he lashed out at Lee:

> "I'm so sick of hearing about damn Spike Lee.
>
> Spike can go straight to hell! You can print that. I am sick of him talking about me, I am sick of him saying, 'this is a coon, this is a buffoon.' I am sick of him talking about black people going to see movies. This is what he said: 'you vote by what you see,' as if black people don't know what they want to see.
>
> I am sick of him – he talked about Whoopi, he talked about Oprah, he talked about me, he talked about Clint Eastwood. Spike needs to shut the hell up!
>
> I've never seen Jewish people attack Seinfeld and say "this is a stereotype," I've never seen Italian people attack The Sopranos, I've never seen Jewish people complaining about *Mrs. Doubtfire* or Dustin Hoffman in *Tootsie*. I never saw it. It's always black people, and this is something that I cannot undo. Booker T. Washington and W.E.B. DuBois went through the exact same thing."

Fighting off oppressors and standing up for what is right is important. It is the very principle that led to the founding of our nation.

[10] Mancini, Vince. "Tyler Perry Says Spike Lee Can Go To hell." FilmDrunk. N.p., 20 Apr. 2011. Web.

With that said, it is important to discriminate between the battles that need to be fought and the battles that are simply being fought because they promote a culture that is different from the standard. The last portion of Perry's quote is telling. It is difficult to find another race or creed that places a negative connotation on success. You can find it in some religious settings (Jehovah's Witnesses for example. They have rules against higher education and wealth. Coincidentally, 37% of JWs are African-American [11]), but rarely to the extent that it exists in the black community.

Unless an African-American acquires wealth through athletics, the lottery, or illegal operations, there is a contingent that will consider him or her an Uncle Tom.This mindset is a classic example of "cutting off the nose to spite the face." Successful patterns are to be mimicked and copied, not avoided. Grant Hill's Duke team beat Michigan and the *Fab Five* handily by a score of 71-51. Both teams had talented players, but Duke was well coached and fundamentally sound. The free-styled approach that Michigan used was no match for the game plan that Duke put into place. That team was willing to do what it took to succeed. They relied on a proven method and it worked.

If the impoverished community is to see more success, they are going to have to *want* to be successful. It is going to be important for them to rally around other successful people in the community. Shaming harmful behaviors and applauding achievement need to be the norm. Currently, much of the poorer community has a very small window in which it can enjoy success. The odds are not great to win the lottery or become a professional athlete. It is almost impossible to make a living from crime as you will eventually end up in jail. Using the methods to success that are proven and timeless will work for them. Hard work, education, and strong life-choices need to be goals that are promoted within the community before it is able to crack through its self-inflicted ceiling.

[11] "Demographics of Jehovah's Witnesses." Wikipedia. N.p., N.d. Web.

Chapter 17

What's In a Name?

As I mentioned in Chapter 5, Na'Licia created a unique social experiment of her own by naming her children. The consensus opinion is that it can be more difficult for someone with an exotic name to get a job or interview than someone with a more traditional name. My goal for this topic (and book) is not to take a political stance or to be judgmental. I simply want to look at the trends and facts to pinpoint areas where poor communities can make positive steps that break the generational cycles of poverty. A name can indicate a lot about a person, but does a name control that person's destiny?

The odds have been stacked against all of Na'Licia's children. They were born to a single, teenaged mother who lives in project housing. Still, does one child have an advantage over the other two? The prevailing theory is that the child with a more traditional name (Herman) will have the better chance at success. The other two children (Na'Dricia and Deondros) will have one more headwind to deal with because of their names.

Steven D. Levitt and Stephen J. Dubner wrote an amazing book titled *Freakonomics: A Rogue Economist Explores the Hidden Side of Everything*[1]. In that book, they examine this very subject. Their first example is almost unbelievable. A father living in Harlem named two of his children "Winner" and "Loser." While neither name is traditional, one would think that "Loser" would be an impossible name to carry around while pursuing a successful life. However, he did. "Lou" became a successful police officer while Winner has a long criminal record.

As we discussed in the previous chapter, the uniqueness of a name coincides with the attitude of contradicting things that are *white.* Levitt and Dubner took California baby names from the '60s through the '90s and compared the likelihood of a "black" girl's name (a name that is more likely to be used by African-Americans) being given to a white, girl baby. The trends were incredible. In 1970, a black girl's name was about twice as common to land with a black child versus a white child. In 1980, that name was 20 times more likely to

[1] Levitt, Steven D., and Stephen J. Dubner. "Freakonomics: A Rogue Economist Explores the Hidden Side of Everything." Harper Perennial, 25 Aug. 2009. Web.

be given to a black child. In 1990, the trend exploded to a likelihood of 100,000 to 1. The authors drive home the point by stating, "Even more remarkably, nearly 30 percent of the black girls are given a name that is unique among every baby, white and black, born that year in California. (There were also 228 babies named Unique during the 1990s alone, and one each of Uneek, Uneque, and Uneqqee; virtually all of them were black)."

The conclusion to this phenomenon is certainly debatable because there are several reasonable assumptions that can be made.Why is it possible to send two similar resumes to a potential employer with different names at the top and see only the traditional name get a call-back? Is it blatant racism or is it a deduction from the employer that the interviewee with the exotic name comes from a less-desirable situation? According to Levitt and Dubner:

> "The data show that, on average, a person with a distinctively black name—whether it is a woman named Imani or a man named DeShawn—does have a worse life outcome than a woman named Molly or a man named Jake. But it isn't the fault of his or her name. If two black boys, Jake Williams and DeShawn Williams, are born in the same neighborhood and into the same familial and economic circumstances, they would likely have similar life outcomes. But the kind of parents who name their son Jake don't tend to live in the same neighborhoods or share economic circumstances with the kind of parents who name their son DeShawn. And that's why, on average, a boy named Jake will tend to earn more money and get more education than a boy named DeShawn. DeShawn's name is an indicator—but not a cause—of his life path."

Most believe that a person bearing a unique name will outperform a person with a traditional name if they have a better education, supportive parents, and wealth. This commentary would support the authors of *Freakonomics.* A name may be an indicator of your background, but it does not control your destiny. Still, not everyone believes in this idea. Meghan Daum examines the link between a name and success in life in her *Los Angeles Times* article *Doomed by your name* [2]?. She references a Shippensburg University study that

[2] Daum, Meghan. "Doomed by Your Name?" Los Angeles Times. N.p., N.d. Web. 7 Feb. 2009.

assigned an index to names based on popularity in the late '80s and early '90s. Daum writes:

> "The Shippensburg researchers first assigned a popularity score to boys' names, based on how often they showed up in birth records in an undisclosed state from 1987 to 1991. Michael, the No. 1 boy's name, had a Popular Name Index score of 100; names such as Malcolm and Preston had index scores of 1. The researchers then assessed names of young men born during that time who landed in the juvenile justice system. They found that only half had a rating higher than 11. By comparison, in the general population, half of the names scored higher than 20. The take-away? "A 10% increase in the popularity of a name is associated with a 3.7% decrease in the number of juvenile delinquents who have that name."

Impoverished communities certainly do not have the market cornered on unique or odd names. Meghan Daum points out that "A lot of baby names in Hollywood these days would have to rate negative PNI scores. I'm not just talking about marginally weird names like Gwyneth Paltrow's daughter's name, Apple, or Sylvester Stallone's son, Sage Moonblood. I'm talking names like Pilot Inspektor (actor Jason Lee's son), Hud and Speck Wildhorse (singer John Mellencamp's sons), and Tu (actor Rob Morrow's daughter; get it? Tu Morrow?)." Regardless, with the immense success of the parents, these exotically named children have a significant advantage in life over just about all of us.

Still, the theme remains the same; children with unique names come from a parent that is expressing a form of individuality. While we encourage this trait in most children, it is not always admired by the corporate world. Many jobs look for someone that is going to conform to policy, follow the rules, and be a team player. While Herman may sound like the type that might fit these various conventions, employers may have their doubts about Deondros.

As I mentioned before, I have a white friend that is married to a Thai woman. Coincidentally, I also have a white brother-in-law that is married to a Thai woman. My friend named his children Xander and Liam and hyphenated the last name. While the first names are somewhat uncommon, they can still use their more formal names, Alexander and William, on resumes. They can also use the Thai last name of the mother when in Thailand and the American father's last name when in the States. My brother-in-law and his wife used one traditional, American name and one Thai name for their child.

Their baby's first name is Savannah and middle name is Tasane. This arrangement was not accidental. Jamelle Bouie of TheDailyBeast.com makes a point that this trend is not isolated to black people. His article *Are Black Names 'Weird,' or Are You Just Racist*? states [3]:

> "But black children aren't the only ones with unusual names. It's not hard to find white kids with names like Braelyn and Declyn. And while it's tempting to chalk this up to poverty—in the Reddit thread, there was wide agreement that this was a phenomenon of poor blacks and poor whites—the wealthy are no strangers to unique names. The popular Netflix show Orange is the New Black, written by a Jenji Kohan (a white woman), was based on the experiences of a Piper Kerman (also a white woman). And in last year's presidential election, nearly 61 million people voted for a Willard Mitt Romney, at the same time that the current head of the Republican National Committee was (and is) a Reince Priebus."

Boule finds the focus on black names to be an illustration of our society's treatment of the African-American community as inferior. He gives this example:

> "They underscore the extent to which our ideas of normality are tied closely to socioeconomic status. If we focus on "weird" African American names in jokes and conversation, it's because blacks remain at the bottom of America's racial caste system. "Hunter" is just as unusual as "Malik," but it's understood as "normal" because of its association with white men. It's arbitrary, yes, but it reflects who holds power. Indeed, if the situation were reversed, odds are good there would be plenty of jokes about "dysfunctional" white people who name their children "Geoff." "

To Mr. Bouie's credit, my wife and I have found many of his contentions to be true. We both come from similar backgrounds, working-class white people. While we moved often, my parents ended up in

[3] Bouie, Jamelle. "Are Black Names 'Weird,' or Are You Just Racist?" The Daily Beast. N.p., 13 Sept. 2013. Web.

an affluent part of the Nashville area in my final years of high school. My wife is from a more rural community in northern Georgia. She has many friends from her hometown that did not go to college and had children immediately after (or during) high school. She has told me about baby names from that community that fit Jamelle Bouie's exact description.

My wife also has the burden of spelling her name every time she meets someone new. She is now cursed by my Hungarian last name, Vass Gal. Vass means "iron", but the "Gal" part is a suffix given to denote a certain region. I think every one of my family members spells it differently. I have seen hyphens between the two words and accents over one or both 'A's. While Vass is common in Hungary and the suffix proves to be useful to denote a certain region over another, there may be no need for the distinctive suffix in this country. Future generations of Vass Gals may rebel against the two-word last name.

To exacerbate her last name issues, my wife's first name is Lyrad. Her father, Daryl Leon, gave her his first and middle name *backwards*. My wife, Lyrad Noel Vass Gal, certainly has a unique name. However, a strong support system, her incredible work-ethic, and brilliance have made her extremely successful. Her brother's name is Drew. Drew is not short for Andrew. He was actually named after an Atlanta Hawks basketball player named John Drew. Both are very impressive individuals. Lyrad has her master's degree (which would be a PhD at most schools) in physical therapy and Drew is an aeronautical engineer.

So, does the name even matter?It is clear that people with exotic names can be successful in life. While true, a name can present an obstacle for a person. While engineers, those with science-based master's degrees, and the inherently rich will be fine with an obscure name, others may not be so fortunate. My focus is more on the people struggling with poverty and their attempt at upward mobility. Is this segment of the population making economic progress more difficult by using unique first names?

Unfortunately, the answer appears to be yes. National Bureau of Economic Research (NBER) Faculty Research Fellows Marianne Bertrand and Sendhil Mullainathan conducted an experiment on the matter [4]. David R. Francis of the NBER wrote about their expe-

[4] Francis, David R. "Employers' Replies to Racial Names." Employers' Replies to Racial Names. The National Bureau of Economic Research, N.d. Web.

riences. Bertrand and Mullainathan

> "sent resumes with either African-American or white-sounding names and then measured the number of call-backs each resume received for interviews. Thus, they experimentally manipulated perception of race via the name on the resume. Half of the applicants were assigned African-American names that are 'remarkably common' in the black population, the other half white sounding names, such as Emily Walsh or Greg Baker."

They sent 5,000 resumes throughout Boston and Chicago for approximately 1,300 position postings. They had some intriguing results. Whites typically had to send 10 resumes to get a callback compared to blacks who had to send 15 resumes. While this discrepancy has statistical significance, Bertrand and Mullainathan found that being white was worth about eight years of experience to level the playing field for person with a black-sounding name.

I found many similar studies conducted in the same manner. I liked this one in particular because of its large sample size. It clearly states the difficulty of applying for a job with a nontraditional name. We can call that phenomenon "racism" and "discrimination," but it is important to accept that this correlation exists. I certainly do not advocate this form of discrimination when deciding among job applicants, but it does occur. While those conducting interviews should look at education and experience, it is clear that they are also looking at names.

While many prefer to focus on the fairness of our various social constructs, I do not always feel that it is a productive exercise. I find myself looking at more practical measures and applications. When it comes to names, I agree that it is not fair to face discrimination. The victim did not even have a voice in the matter. Most times, their parent(s) chose the name.

An obscure name can make a life more challenging.While an unfair practice, interviewers look at the entire resume. It is incredibly difficult to know what kind of person they are getting by looking at a piece of paper full of achievements. When there are too many applicants to interview, the weeding-out process can be unfair. They are looking for any excuse to remove a name from the list and narrow the field of applicants.

Why is there a perception that black names are inherently less qualified that white names? That seems to be a blatantly racist observation in itself. It is and that may be the reason that some interviewers discard a resume. Racism certainly exists. Still, there are other reasons that also contribute to this practice in name discrimination. Fair or not, obscure names lead to other conclusions. The most obvious is that the person comes from a poor area and is the product of an unstable home. An odd name also provokes the thought that the applicant may come from a privileged life and has parents that have coddled him or her too much. There are also many employers that would rather not hire a foreigner. Many foreign students change their first names in the United States for this reason.

It is a social injustice and certainly worth a fight. Na'Dricia and Deondros should have the exact same opportunity for success as Herman. Nevertheless, being defiant in naming a child has negative consequences that present the same challenges as the Uncle Tom issue. Leading your own life and making your own decisions is important. For that reason, it is vital to know the implications of these decisions. If someone is going to choose a distinctive name for his or her child, it could result in that person being passed over for a job, college, or other competitive application process. Most parents want to give their children every advantage possible. Unfortunately, statistics show that unique names close doors and create unnecessary challenges.

Chapter 18

Program Results and Impressions

My relationship with Jermaine was worth my time, money, and effort on its own. Joining a program like Big Brothers Big Sisters or otherwise volunteering time to a child is incredibly rewarding. Children are extraordinarily perceptive and impressionable. Being a solid role model can give them the example they need to improve their lives. Little changes and alterations in behavior are so satisfying to witness. It is a great feeling to see an underprivileged child make positive steps and know that you directly contributed to their progress.

I would love to have seen Jermaine go to college and become a doctor or something remarkable. That would have been the ultimate success story.However, I was unprepared for what I was getting into and did not have a proper plan of action in place. There are several things I would have done differently. Still, he has turned into a fine young man that loves his family and is responsible enough to care for those around him. While I admire his loyalty, I am saddened by the limitations that this situation has created for his life.

If someone is interested in working with BBBS, he or she will need to be prepared for the pressures that a young person has in an impoverished community. Influences come from many different directions. School, church, and family all perpetuate a way of life. Even when many people mean well with their guidance, they may be ignorant to the behaviors that are needed to be consistently successful. It is challenging for a child to sort through advice that comes from loved ones to know what is good and what is bad. When a trusted adult steers a kid in a certain direction, it is extremely difficult for them to delineate from that path.

For that reason, parenting is incredibly important in the development of a child. If a parent is unprepared, then the child will suffer. This is the very root of the generational nature of poverty. Every other challenge is secondary. There is a reason that wealth can quickly disappear when it is inherited, just as there is a reason that two hard-working, poor parents can raise a successful child. The developmental years are critical and must be nourished properly. While there are isolated stories where children are able to grow up and buck these trends, it is not common.

Studying behavioral tendencies is a growing segment within the economics community. While human behavior in large numbers has been the foundation for most historical assumptions, it can also be quite useful when looking at more microeconomic situations. Economists tend to be more exacting when looking at difficult human conditions. It can be quite difficult for most people (economists included) to look at people facing poverty and make an educated suggestion of how to treat the problem. The kneejerk reaction is to have the government throw money at the problem. It is the most passive response and spreads the responsibility among a large group of people.

This sounds reasonable, but does it work? This is where economists and other number crunchers become valuable.Defining a quantifiable benefit to the money being spent is important. Otherwise, we are spending money to make ourselves feel better with no real regard to helping those in need. It becomes more of a superficial approach and not one that creates a meaningful and lasting change. That is my goal and should be our goal as a country. I want to find a way to create a permanent improvement in the life and culture of our more impoverished communities.

That cultural shift begins with parents and is most important for shaping their children. We have to find a way to make success the goal and only option. How do we do that? How do we take the melancholy nature that has developed within the poor community and transform it into one that sharpens young people into promising students and productive adults? To make this progress, strong leaders will need to emerge and become difference makers within their communities.

It is clear that it does take a village to develop the necessary culture that is conducive to proper childhood development. Unfortunately, in lower-income communities there are consistent cultural flaws that prevent the "villagers" from advancing in life. While one-on-one interactions with a child can make important differences in his or her life, real and sustainable traction will only come from communities rearranging their priorities.

Stating this necessity sounds simplistic, but putting the measures into place to accomplish consistent advancement is certainly complicated.Somehow, the mindset must be changed. Is this something we can do at the national level through taxes and educational programs or does it need to be a more grass-roots effort? I have my doubts about throwing tax dollars at problems and expecting behavioral changes. Real improvements come from strong leadership and willing followers.

As we have discussed throughout this book, impoverished communities will need to learn and utilize the common traits of those who are consistently successful. More leaders will need to step to the forefront and lobby for these changes in attitude. It is not easy, but it is necessary. The efforts of Bill Cosby and Martin Luther King, Jr. were crucial in the advancement of African-Americans. More leaders will need to emerge and the majority of them will be less renowned. Parents, followed by religious leaders and teachers have the capability of shaping their communities.

The first alteration of perception needs to come from avoiding all things considered being *white*. I can understand the rebellious attitude. It results from the heartbreaking years of slavery and the staunch racism that exists today. Still, "being white" is a label applied to many of the initiatives that make one successful. Avoiding these items is not accomplishing its intended purpose.To make the more racist side of white-America uncomfortable, black success in academia and business would be the most effective.

To make this transition, attitudes must change. It has to be acceptable and encouraged to speak traditional English. Communities must stop praising teenage pregnancies and young parenthood. Gangs and prison cannot be an acceptable alternative. Rebelliousness has to be tempered and conformity accepted. The idea that the pursuit of wealth or knowledge is selling-out is a cancer that must be removed.

The problem with the shift is clear, but wealthy, white people do not have the monopoly on fortune. It is open to everyone, but success is unlikely to change its prerequisites. A person will have to have the ability to conform. He or she will have to fit the model that many poor people despise. An individual that speaks clearly, listens, follows directions, is flexible, is clean, shows consistency with work history and grades, and generally steers clear of the more dramatic elements in life will have opportunities. There is a general shortage of people that fit that description.

While government assistance will probably not help much with this issue, work programs and community centers can.Organizations that give personal attention to at-risk young adults and children can make a difference. I would prefer to see more money sent to an organization like the Boys & Girls Club and less allocated for welfare. One program really works to develop marketable skills that can be used throughout an individual's life while the other makes poverty a reasonable life alternative.

The most ambitious idea would be to eliminate all welfare. This idea seems cold and would never make it through Congress (or be a popular platform for any politician), but it would be effective in shrinking the poor population. Taxes would drop and that would cause an economic stimulus by itself. Anyone that could work would now have every incentive to do so.

The real leap of faith from a movement like this would be to trust in the local community to care for their poor without government help. Churches would have to be instrumental in this transformation. Given enough time, the economic growth from less social spending would hopefully employ people that had never considered working. This would cause a natural decline in the number of impoverished citizens as well as increase the number of taxpayers.

While this option has potential, it is unrealistic. It is too precarious for most voters to take seriously. Seeing someone in absolute poverty is upsetting and pushing through an agenda that pulls tax money from that person comes across as callous and selfish. Most people want to help the poor, but they do not want to actually spend much time with the poor. Giving money (and asking for others to give money) is much more convenient and it helps us to avoid getting our hands dirty.

When you combine the unwillingness of most people to work with the less fortunate and the unwillingness of the less fortunate to work toward a better life, you have a problem. I can understand the former's attitude. It can be tough to insert volunteer work into a person's busy schedule. However, I was most surprised to find the latter attitude existed.Many poor people are content. They would certainly prefer to get more money from the government, but they can also make do with their current allotment. Even in poverty, many people can still find comfort in conforming to their society's standard.

After my interview with Jermaine's family, I looked for some local jobs for him. I found one with United Parcel Service (UPS) and sent a link to him on Facebook. I have a client that retired from UPS and is a millionaire. He was a driver that worked hard and saved aggressively. It is a great company. Jermaine told me that he could not work because he was currently on disability and that working might jeopardize his government payments.

I countered by asking him to check into that. He might be able to work a few hours and still receive his benefits. I also mentioned to him that companies do hire people with disabilities. In fact, sometimes they look for disabled workers to fill quotas. I advised him to check into the job and be honest about his Crohn's disease. Jermaine told me that he would check it out, but I feel like he was just being polite. I do not expect him to follow through with it.

While I will continue to work on Jermaine, his Uncle Aaron gave me some great news recently. Aaron was accepted to Alabama A&M for college. He is a bright, hard-working young man and it was wonderful to see his efforts payoff. One would clearly have to give his mother the credit for his development. She was strict with his upbringing and he had no choice, but to be successful. He stayed out of trouble and met his schooling obligations consistently. I told him to contact me with any and all college questions that he might have. Aaron is breaking the mold and has a real shot at changing the generational trajectory of his family. I expect Aaron to get more college offers before he has to make a decision.

I have also seen some real improvement with my wife's Little Sister, Erika. Erika comes from a similar background as Jermaine. She has a father in prison, but lives with her grandmother. Her mother does not see her often as she is typically on drugs and exhibits other irresponsible behaviors. Erika has been the middleman in drug deals for her mother and is in a much better situation with her grandmother.

When Lyrad first met Erika, she was a feisty child. She had many preconceived notions about the man in a relationship paying for everything and that she would find a man who would do that for her. To me, being around Erika was largely unpleasant. I believe this was something that she developed at school. However, through the years, she has matured and has a much better attitude. I know that her grandmother would not tolerate that kind of behavior at home.

Now, Erika is very sweet and well-mannered young woman. She avoids her mother and the other bad influences in her family and does well in school. I expect that Erika will also go to college. Even with the considerable obstacles in her life, she has had enough good influences to contradict normal trends. Her grandmother is extremely proud of Erika and has done a great job in raising her. Lyrad has also been an amazing influence and Erika knows that she can confide in her.

From my experience, the nature versus nurture argument is an easy one to conclude. As one moves toward the law of large numbers, nurture starts to win.The comparisons of children that come from a supporting family versus a neglectful one are night and day. Children develop better when they are disciplined and receive attention during their developmental years. A neglected child that comes from a wealthy home has a better chance of being successful than a neglected child from a poorer household. Still, the child that gets consistent attention, regardless of his or her rung on the socio-economic ladder, is the one most likely to maximize his or her potential.

While parenting is the most critical piece in a child's development, community development can play a significant factor. A child's friends, family, church, and community give them important examples of how their life should unfold. Their actions serve as a guideline. Children learn racism, expectations, methodology, what is possible, how to communicate, and ultimately what they will find to be normal from their surroundings. If *normal* is success, then a child with a supportive home will probably be successful. If that normal is government assistance, then that is an unfortunate scenario that is likely to be repeated.

While the challenge is significant, improvements can and must be made. Organizations like Big Brothers Big Sisters do a great job of providing underprivileged children with hope. Still, more needs to be done within the community. Churches and schools are an integral part in the lives of many people and they provide a speaking platform for community leaders. This is important because that platform needs to be utilized. More community leaders must step forward in impoverished communities. They must challenge and push those around them to make better choices.

I found my work with Jermaine to be frustrating and rewarding at the same time. I would encourage anyone that wants to make a difference in the life of a child to pursue a program like BBBS.Volunteers will need to realize what they will be up against, and that the odds may not be in their favor. The good news is that the parent has made a choice to try to improve his or her child's life. The mother, father, grandmother, grandfather, aunt, uncle, or sibling is admitting that they need help and that is an important first step. Still, clear guidelines and goals must be established in the beginning between the guardian and Big to make discernable progress.

For a family living in poverty, many times, it only takes one successful family member to make an impact that can last for generations. Success is contagious. Once the first family member goes to college, it is likely that his or her children will go to college. The family learns what it takes to maneuver around the obstacles of life. They then share that knowledge with their children. This trajectory is extremely difficult to change; just as it is tough to alter the cyclical nature of poverty. However, it takes time, patience, and strong leadership within the community to move away from a culture of failure and embrace the qualities that make one successful.

While working through this book, I did not want to paint a picture that had an agenda or was overly optimistic. My goal was to give an accurate portrayal of my experience and then critique some of the challenges that the poor face as they relate to economic philosophy. I do not feel that my experience is unique from many that try a program like BBBS. In fact, I know that many Bigs quit early in the process. It can be incredibly unsatisfying at times. You find yourself wanting to help this child so badly and your efforts are continually spoiled by your Little's friends and family.

With that said, there are success stories—a lot of them. Bigs do make a difference for many of the children involved. That difference just varies in degree depending on that individual's experience. Everyone that is willing to sign up as a big must be ready for a challenge. However, any incremental change you create for a child will make the entire experience worthwhile.

I would like to see this subject become more popular within the economics community. While interest rate movements, inflation, and GDP fluctuations are important for the working community, the growth of the impoverished community should be a more pressing concern. That growth not only creates a struggle for that particular group, but it also creates a tax expense for the workers of the country. Everyone is impacted and everyone would benefit from its progression.

Because economists use a steady recipe of math and art (many economics degrees are a BA) when dissecting an issue, you will get many different suggestions as to how to combat poverty. The traditional approach of increasing taxes and increasing the scope of our social programs is ineffective. While this method does provide much needed comfort to some, it also expands the number of individuals using those programs.

Our future financial success as a country will depend on economists rolling up their sleeves and addressing our growing poverty trends. It is a complex issue and will need to continue to be studied from the inside. We need to find methods that produce incentives for individuals to discontinue the legacies created by their parents and grandparents. This process will not be easy and the answers will probably not be simple. Like a scientist working to treat cancer, it will be important to try different treatments.Some will work, but many will not. Still, *curing* poverty is a worthwhile pursuit and the continued development of our country depends on us finding resolutions.

Appendix: Poverty Around the World

When examining poverty in an otherwise wealthy nation, it is reasonable to formulate plans to eliminate that condition. After all, we have already shown that the likelihood of economic mobility is greater when a poor person or family is surrounded by wealthy people. However, many parts of the world do not have this same opportunity. Europe, Africa, and South America have large sections of impoverished people who are surrounded by other impoverished people. Many of them face corrupt governments and are born into a situation that provides little hope. As Americans, we have been quick to notice these hardships and to provide financial assistance.

It has been said that foreign aid is the transfer of funds from poor people in rich countries to rich people in poor countries. Unfortunately, there is some truth in that idea. Like any government program, foreign aid is run through taxation and funded through the efforts of the working class. While many citizens are happy to help those in need, it can be difficult to appreciate the fruits of their charity. The intent of foreign aid seems to be corrupted by political capital and other various agendas. While some money does reach its intended target, it is difficult to find actual progress in the more impoverished nations of the world as a result of our giving.

To get some insight into this situation, I am referring to a man that has experienced the extreme poverty that our world has to offer. Ed Colvin's mission work and kindness has made him an expert in this arena. I put together a series of questions regarding the efforts of the American taxpayer. Are we truly making a difference with our funding or do we need more "boots on the ground" to attack global poverty?

Talk about your travels a bit and your mission.

"Project C.U.R.E. is a non-profit 501©3 that is a para-church organization functioning in partnership with churches in support of the mission work of their denomination. The ministry of Project C.U.R.E. is providing donated medical equipment and supplies through missionaries to show God's love in tangible practical ways. My travel took me to twenty-eight countries in what is considered the developing world. We resource medical professionals with tools they do not have to treat the people who have no hope."

"This is done as part of a strategic plan developed by going to the country, living with the people and the missionary, visiting hospitals, clinics and jungle outposts, and learning how medicine is practiced there. What resources do they have now? Where and how are the medical providers trained? We assess their ability to use technology. Do they have the basic supplies like gloves, suture, stethoscopes, and sterile supplies? Do they have electricity? How is it generated? How dependable is it? Do they clean water? What is its source? We would watch the provider perform surgeries, visit and treat patients, asking questions as we go. Gradually you earn the trust of the provider when they see you are not going to be the 'Ugly American' coming to tell them what they are doing wrong and correct them. Pictures are taken to document their story." "Each facility visited has its own strategic plan which is developed in cooperation with the medical professionals working there and reviewed with them before we leave their facility. Typically a trip would involve 5-15 needs assessments touching on most spectrums of medical care."

"Needs Assessments are then discussed with local leaders like a village chief, then with the national government. These meetings were to gain cooperation and lay the frame work for an ongoing relationship. The officials of the national government would be visited in person and involved in a discussion about what we were planning to gain their support. First would be the Ministry of Health to review the plans for medical efficacy, cultural appropriateness, and consistency with their national healthcare plan. This is followed by customs officials to learn the laws for shipping items into the country. The final visit is with the country's leader to gain their support and a signed waiver of all customs, duties and tariffs as well as expediting of shipments through customs and if there were security concerns, an armed military escort if needed. The missionary becomes the Project C.U.R.E. accountable partner to the healthcare providers, the government and our organization. We make it clear that if any of the donated material is misappropriated, future shipments cease. This has resulted in not one of the containers failing to reach its intended recipient."

"When I returned to the United States we set to work with a network of volunteers to secure donated surplus medical equipment and supplies. Volunteers inventoried and checked each item to make sure it was fully functional and complete. Fifty-foot ocean containers were then packed with equipment and supplies appropriate for the need. Subsequent containers were progressively geared to develop their ability to handle technology. Typically, what resulted were facilities that could stand on their own and in many cases micro economic enterprises developed sharing one facility's capabilities with others or selling services at nominal cost to sustain the level of care.

What example(s) of poverty caught your eye and left the most lasting impression?

"Much of the world is comprised of two basic economic strata: the wealthy and the desperately poor. Governments are corrupt and view people as disposable. The poor have little hope of their situations ever getting better so they learn to be content. The majority of the world's healthcare could be greatly improved by clean water, proper sanitary hygiene, and a nutritious diet. There are regionally specific factors that also enter into the picture such as insect borne diseases, water borne parasites, insecticide poisoning, environmental caused respiratory issues. Each place I visited had its unique health issues but the basics water, diet and sanitation were universal."

"A large percentage of the poor people in these countries would love to be homeless in America. Their personal situation would be vastly improved. Americans have no concept of real poverty."

What are impoverished people doing that keep them in poverty generation after generation?

"They see no way for their circumstances to ever improve. They become resigned to their circumstance. Few pursue advancing their education. They are caught up in a cycle where hard work means you have enough to sometimes feed your family today. The poor view economics as a barter system at best."

What would be the best way to move impoverished people and nations forward?

"Certainly not United States foreign aid, which ends up in the hands of the corrupt and greedy rulers. The church is another option to provide assistance to the poor. NGO's teaching them how to improve at a more local level and providing initial resources to get them started. This does not necessarily mean money. Project C.U.R.E. uses surplus medical equipment and supplies from our healthcare system's excess. It is amazing what can be accomplished when no one seeks the credit. I believe that practical education is a key element of raising the poor from their poverty. Teaching them how to increase the yield for their effort and then how to apply and share that knowledge and success with others. Starting microeconomic projects will teach them to grow with dignity."

"This progress will be gradual. It cannot happen by redistributing wealth, nor from handouts. That simply results in dependence and leads to a different type of despair and hopelessness. People and nations must be allowed a sense of accomplishment with an underlying dignity."

Please elaborate on your feelings about American taxation for global aid. Is it not effective?

"No, it is not. Governments of impoverished countries are often a major contributing factor to the poverty. Corruption is rampant with in the government. Foreign Aid is misappropriated to themselves or their cohorts or supporters."

"I have seen this first hand on numerous occasions when speaking with heads of state about Project C.U.R.E. One of the first questions they ask is what is in it for them. It takes significant effort and creative thinking to convince them of the benefit when no bribes are paid."

Do the impoverished people of this country face the same obstacles as those you encountered in your travels? Are there any noticeable differences in those two groups?

"Although I lived among the impoverished indigenous people and experienced their lives, both they and I knew I would eventually go home. I was frequently asked why I would leave the comfort and ease of life in the U.S. which provided a segway to explaining exactly why I was there." "There are notable differences between the people encountered–because you saw the wealthy and their abundance beside the desperately poor. There were modern private hospitals and healthcare available to those who could pay. Everyone else was disposable and forgotten."

Do you feel that you made a lasting difference with your work? What are some success stories you have enjoyed?

"The work I was privileged to share in has had dramatic and lasting impact. People have a much higher quality of healthcare available. Methods have been developed to sustain, expand, and grow the healthcare in surrounding areas."

"My last project involved a West African country. Corruption and violence are rampant in this country. The people are desperately poor even though the country is rich in natural resources. I witnessed surgeries performed under what we would call barbaric circumstances; clinics with virtually nothing to care for the sick and dying. People who came to the doctor or nurse seeking some kind of relief only to find no medicine, or resources to treat them. Basic items, even disposable gloves were unheard of. If they had gloves, they were reused time and again. There was no laboratory equipment, durable medical supplies, certainly no diagnostic equipment."

"A few months after conducting Needs Assessments and developing a strategic plan, the first containers of basic medical supplies arrived. These resourced clinics and regional health centers progressively granting them greater and greater capabilities. The end of the first year of our relationship was marked with the opening of a new hospital which Project C.U.R.E. equipped. This included the only dialysis unit in that part of the country, CAT scan, MRI, Operating rooms, X-Ray, hospital beds, basically everything needed to operate the hospital. The items were donated from the surplus of the Nashville healthcare community. The hospital is now the teaching hospital for that part of the country. Countless people have enjoyed better health and longer lives. This was made possible by God and the local missionaries seeking to do ministry and when necessary use words. It is also significant to note that Project C.U.R.E. receives no government funding and none of our projects are government controlled. People helping people to elevate themselves allowing them dignity and respect."

Acknowledgements

I want to thank "Jermaine" and his family. They have always been kind to me and I appreciate them allowing me into their lives. I hope that I have been a positive influence as I have certainly learned a great deal from them. Chastity, Tremaine, Na'Licia, Aaron, and Jermaine are wonderful, caring people and I wish them the absolute best.

My wife, Lyrad, continues to support my endeavors and is a great Big Sister. She has been a strong mentor to her Little and I am very proud of what she has been able to accomplish with Erika. It will be a joy to watch her graduate from high school and enter college.

Vernon Press has been wonderful to work with on this project. It has been a thrill to have such an attentive publisher take notice of my work. They have been consummate professionals.

I want to express gratitude to my contributor, Ed Colvin. He was not only gracious enough to allow me to interview him, but his work is instrumental in the world's progression out of poverty.

I am so impressed by all of the people around the world that are getting their hands dirty and working directly in impoverished conditions. They are the ones making a real difference. Giving your time is a great sacrifice, but it makes the most significant impact.

Index

CPSIA information can be obtained at www.ICGtesting.com
Printed in the USA
LVOW06*2152211115

463306LV00006B/14/P